World's Oldest Structures: Famous Landmarks of the Ancient Times

Shah Rukh

Published by Shah Rukh, 2024.

While every precaution has been taken in the preparation of this book, the publisher assumes no responsibility for errors or omissions, or for damages resulting from the use of the information contained herein.

WORLD'S OLDEST STRUCTURES: FAMOUS LANDMARKS OF THE ANCIENT TIMES

First edition. July 23, 2024.

Copyright © 2024 Shah Rukh.

Written by Shah Rukh.

Table of Contents

Prologue

In the vast tapestry of human history, certain landmarks stand as enduring testaments to the ingenuity, creativity, and resilience of our ancestors. These ancient structures, some weathered by millennia yet still imposing, whisper stories of civilizations long past. They are the remnants of human endeavor, the physical embodiments of cultural and historical narratives that have shaped our world.

"World's Oldest Structures: Famous Landmarks of the Ancient Times" invites you on a journey through time, exploring the most iconic and mysterious ancient edifices ever constructed. Each chapter is a portal into a different epoch, offering a glimpse into the lives, beliefs, and aspirations of those who came before us.

From the majestic Great Pyramid of Giza, standing sentinel over the sands of Egypt, to the enigmatic stone circles of Stonehenge in England, these structures reveal the remarkable capabilities of early engineers and architects. They speak of societies that, despite lacking modern technology, achieved feats of construction and artistry that continue to awe and inspire.

As you delve into the stories behind these ancient wonders, you will uncover the diverse motivations that drove their creation. Some were built to honor deities and house the divine, like the awe-inspiring Temple of Karnak. Others served as centers of governance and social organization, such as the grand Acropolis of Athens. Still, others remain shrouded in mystery, their true purposes lost to the sands of time, inviting endless speculation and wonder.

These structures are more than mere buildings; they are monuments to human ambition and imagination. They remind us of the profound connections that bind us to our past and highlight the universal human desire to create, to endure, and to leave a legacy.

In these pages, you will not only encounter the architectural marvels of ancient civilizations but also the stories of the people who built them. From the laborers who toiled in the shadow of the Great Wall of China to the priests who presided over the sacred rites at the Temple of Artemis, each structure is a chapter in the grand saga of humanity.

Join us as we traverse the globe and the annals of history, visiting the world's oldest and most famous landmarks. May this exploration ignite your curiosity, deepen your appreciation for our shared heritage, and inspire a newfound wonder for the ancient times.

Welcome to a journey through the timeless, the magnificent, and the enduring. Welcome to "World's Oldest Structures: Famous Landmarks of the Ancient Times."

Chapter 1: Great Pyramid of Giza

The Great Pyramid of Giza, also known as the Pyramid of Khufu or the Pyramid of Cheops, is a monumental structure that stands as a testament to the ingenuity, ambition, and architectural prowess of ancient Egyptian civilization. Located on the Giza Plateau near Cairo, Egypt, it is the largest of the three pyramids in the Giza pyramid complex and the oldest of the Seven Wonders of the Ancient World. Remarkably, it is the only one of these wonders to have survived to the present day in a relatively intact form. The construction of the Great Pyramid dates back to around 2580–2560 BC, during the Fourth Dynasty of the Old Kingdom of Egypt, and it was built as a tomb for the Pharaoh Khufu (Cheops in Greek). The project is thought to have taken about 20 years to complete, a feat of engineering and organization that remains impressive even by modern standards.

The pyramid originally stood at 146.6 meters (481 feet), but today it is slightly shorter due to the loss of the outer casing stones and the erosion of its apex. It now rises to a height of approximately 138.8 meters (455 feet). The base of the pyramid covers an area of about 13 acres (5.3 hectares), with each side measuring approximately 230.4 meters (756 feet) in length. The precision with which the base was laid out is astounding, with the sides aligned almost perfectly to the cardinal points of the compass. The construction utilized an estimated 2.3 million blocks of limestone and granite, some weighing as much as 80 tons, with the average block weighing around 2.5 tons. The quarrying, transportation, and assembly of these massive stones remain subjects of intense study and speculation among historians and archaeologists.

The pyramid's structure consists of three main chambers: the King's Chamber, the Queen's Chamber, and the Subterranean Chamber. The King's Chamber, located at the heart of the pyramid, is made entirely of red granite and contains a large sarcophagus thought to have housed the mummified remains of Pharaoh Khufu, though no remains were ever found. The Queen's Chamber lies beneath the King's Chamber and is smaller in size, while the Subterranean Chamber, which is unfinished and lies beneath the pyramid, is accessible through a sloping passageway. The precise purpose of the Queen's and Subterranean Chambers is still debated among scholars.

One of the most intriguing aspects of the Great Pyramid is the complex network of passageways and air shafts that crisscross its interior. These include the Grand Gallery, a steeply inclined corridor that leads up to the King's Chamber, and the so-called "air shafts" that extend from the King's and Queen's Chambers to the exterior of the pyramid. These shafts were long thought to have been used for ventilation, but recent theories suggest they may have had astronomical or ceremonial purposes, aligning with specific stars or constellations.

The outer casing of the pyramid was originally made of highly polished Tura limestone, which would have gleamed brilliantly in the sun, making the pyramid visible from many miles away. Most of this casing was removed over the centuries to build other structures, leaving the core masonry exposed. The precision of the stone-cutting and the quality of the workmanship in the casing stones are yet another testament to the advanced engineering skills of the ancient Egyptians.

The construction methods employed in building the Great Pyramid have been the subject of much debate and speculation. While the exact techniques remain unknown, several theories have been proposed, ranging from the use of massive straight or spiral ramps to the employment of counterweights and levers. Some modern experiments and reconstructions have demonstrated that it would have been possible to build the pyramid using the tools and techniques available at the time, though the labor force required and the organizational logistics would have been enormous.

The workforce responsible for building the Great Pyramid is believed to have been composed of a well-organized group of laborers, possibly numbering in the tens of thousands. These workers were likely not slaves, as was once thought, but rather a mix of skilled laborers, craftsmen, and temporary workers who were well-fed and housed in nearby workers' villages. Evidence from these sites suggests that the laborers were provided with food, medical care, and even beer, indicating that their welfare was taken seriously.

The purpose of the Great Pyramid extends beyond its function as a tomb; it is also a symbol of the pharaoh's absolute power and a reflection of the religious beliefs of the ancient Egyptians. The pyramid was part of a larger funerary complex that included temples, smaller pyramids for queens, and a causeway that linked the pyramid to the Nile River. This complex served as a focal point for the religious and ceremonial activities associated with the pharaoh's journey to the afterlife. The alignment of the pyramid with the cardinal points and the inclusion of astronomical elements in its design suggest a deep connection with the cosmos and the Egyptian belief in the pharaoh's divine role.

The Great Pyramid has fascinated people throughout history, inspiring countless studies, theories, and explorations. In ancient times, it was visited by Greek historians such as Herodotus, who wrote about its construction and the supposed use of slave labor, a notion that has since been debunked. During the medieval period, the pyramid was explored by Arab scholars, who contributed to our understanding of its dimensions and internal structure. In modern times, the Great Pyramid has been the subject of extensive archaeological research, including the use of advanced technologies such as ground-penetrating radar, 3D scanning, and robotics to uncover new information about its construction and purpose.

Despite the many discoveries and insights gained over the years, the Great Pyramid of Giza continues to hold many secrets. The recent discovery of previously unknown voids and chambers within the pyramid, using techniques such as muon tomography, suggests that there is still much to learn about this ancient marvel. These ongoing investigations promise to reveal new details about the construction methods, the lives of the workers, and the cultural and religious significance of the pyramid.

The Great Pyramid of Giza stands not only as a remarkable feat of engineering but also as a symbol of the enduring legacy of ancient Egyptian civilization. Its sheer size, precise construction, and enduring mysteries continue to captivate the imagination of people around the world. As we continue to study and explore this ancient wonder, we gain not only a deeper understanding of the people who built it but also an appreciation for the incredible achievements of one of history's most fascinating cultures. The Great Pyramid remains a powerful reminder of humanity's capacity for creativity, innovation, and perseverance, inspiring future generations to explore and understand the wonders of our past.

Chapter 2: Stonehenge

Stonehenge is one of the most iconic and enigmatic prehistoric monuments in the world. Located on Salisbury Plain in Wiltshire, England, it consists of a circular arrangement of massive standing stones, some of which are topped by horizontal lintels, creating a distinctive and instantly recognizable silhouette. The origins, purpose, and construction methods of Stonehenge have fascinated archaeologists, historians, and the public for centuries, leading to a myriad of theories and ongoing research.

The construction of Stonehenge occurred in several phases, spanning approximately 1,500 years from around 3000 BC to 1500 BC. The earliest phase involved the construction of a circular earthwork enclosure, known as the henge, which consisted of a ditch, bank, and entrance causeways. This phase is often referred to as the "earthen henge" and is believed to have been used for ceremonial or ritual purposes, possibly as a burial ground, evidenced by the presence of cremated human remains in some of the early pits and postholes.

The most dramatic and well-known phase of Stonehenge began around 2500 BC when the iconic sarsen stones and smaller bluestones were erected. The sarsen stones, which are a type of sandstone, were sourced from the Marlborough Downs, approximately 20 miles (32 kilometers) to the north of the site. These stones are massive, with some weighing up to 30 tons. The bluestones, smaller in size but equally impressive, were transported from the Preseli Hills in Wales, a distance of about 140 miles (225 kilometers). The transportation of these stones over such vast distances remains one of the great mysteries of Stonehenge, with theories ranging from the use of sledges and rollers to the possibility of transporting them via waterways.

The layout of Stonehenge is a masterpiece of prehistoric engineering and astronomy. The monument consists of a horseshoe arrangement of five trilithons (two vertical stones with a horizontal lintel across the top) at its center, surrounded by a circle of sarsen stones capped with lintels. Outside this circle lies an outer bank and ditch, and beyond these, there are several additional features, including the Avenue, a processional pathway aligned with the summer solstice sunrise, and various barrows or burial mounds. The alignment of Stonehenge with the solstices and other celestial events suggests that it was used as an ancient astronomical observatory, allowing its builders to track the movements of the sun, moon, and stars. This alignment is particularly evident during the summer solstice when the sun rises directly above the Heel Stone, a single large sarsen stone located outside the main circle, casting a beam of light into the center of the monument.

The construction of Stonehenge required an incredible amount of labor and resources. It is estimated that thousands of people would have been involved in the quarrying, transportation, and erection of the stones. This suggests a highly organized and socially complex society with the ability to mobilize and sustain a large workforce. The precise methods used to erect the stones remain a topic of debate, but it is generally believed that they were erected using a combination of earthen ramps, wooden frames, and sheer human strength.

The purpose of Stonehenge has been the subject of much speculation and research. Early theories suggested it was a druid temple, but this idea has been largely discredited since the Druids arrived in Britain long after Stonehenge was built. More recent theories propose that it served multiple purposes over its long history, including as a burial ground, a ceremonial site, a place of healing, and an astronomical observatory. The discovery of human remains and artifacts in and around the site, such as pottery, tools, and animal bones, supports the idea that Stonehenge was a significant ceremonial center where various rituals and activities took place.

One of the most intriguing aspects of Stonehenge is its connection to other nearby prehistoric sites, forming a wider landscape of ancient activity. The Stonehenge Landscape includes other notable features such as the Cursus, a long rectangular earthwork; the Avenue, a processional pathway; and numerous barrows and henges, including Woodhenge and Durrington Walls. These sites, together with Stonehenge, suggest that the area was of immense importance to prehistoric peoples and may have served as a hub for social, religious, and ceremonial gatherings.

The construction of Stonehenge can be divided into several main stages, each contributing to its final form. The first stage, around 3000 BC, involved the construction of the circular earthwork enclosure and the digging of Aubrey Holes, named after the 17th-century antiquarian John Aubrey, who first identified them. These holes, 56 in total, may have held wooden posts or stones and were later repurposed for burials.

The second stage, starting around 2500 BC, saw the erection of the central sarsen stone circle and the inner horseshoe arrangement of trilithons. The sarsen stones were carefully shaped and smoothed, with the lintels jointed to the uprights using a sophisticated mortise and tenon system, demonstrating advanced stone-working techniques. The bluestones were also brought to the site during this period, initially arranged in a double circle and later rearranged into an inner horseshoe and outer circle.

The third stage, around 2300 BC, involved further rearrangements of the bluestones and the addition of more stones to the monument. This period also saw the construction of the Avenue, linking Stonehenge with the River Avon, and the addition of the Heel Stone and Slaughter Stone, both of which are significant for their alignments with celestial events.

Subsequent stages of construction and modification continued until around 1500 BC, with changes to the arrangement of the stones, the addition of more bluestones, and the construction of new features in the surrounding landscape. Each phase of construction reflects changes in the social and religious practices of the people who built and used Stonehenge.

The study of Stonehenge has advanced significantly with the advent of modern archaeological techniques. Excavations, radiocarbon dating, and geophysical surveys have provided new insights into the chronology and construction methods of the monument. For example, recent research has identified the sources of the bluestones in the Preseli Hills and has revealed details about the quarrying and transportation processes. Advanced imaging techniques have also been used to create detailed digital models of the site, allowing for new interpretations of its design and function.

Despite these advances, many questions about Stonehenge remain unanswered. The exact methods used to transport and erect the stones, the specific rituals and activities conducted at the site, and the full extent of its astronomical alignments are still subjects of ongoing research and debate. New discoveries, such as previously unknown burials and artifacts, continue to shed light on the lives and beliefs of the people who built and used Stonehenge.

Stonehenge has long held a special place in British culture and heritage. It has been a source of inspiration for artists, writers, and poets, and has attracted visitors from around the world for centuries. In the 19th and early 20th centuries, it became a focus of conservation efforts, leading to its designation as a protected monument and, in 1986, a UNESCO World Heritage Site. Today, it is managed by English Heritage, which works to preserve and present the site for future generations.

Modern celebrations at Stonehenge, particularly during the summer and winter solstices, reflect its enduring significance as a place of gathering and spiritual reflection. Thousands of people, including modern-day Druids and Pagans, gather to witness the sunrise and sunset, continuing a tradition that dates back millennia. These events highlight the deep connection between Stonehenge and the natural cycles of the year, a connection that was undoubtedly of great importance to its ancient builders.

In recent years, the interpretation and presentation of Stonehenge have been enhanced by the construction of a new visitor center, which provides visitors with information about the history, archaeology, and cultural significance of the site. The center includes exhibitions of artifacts found at Stonehenge and in the surrounding landscape, as well as interactive displays and reconstructions that help to bring the ancient monument to life.

Stonehenge remains a powerful symbol of human ingenuity, creativity, and our enduring fascination with the past. Its construction, involving the coordination of vast resources and labor over many generations, speaks to the social and cultural achievements of the people who built it. As research continues and new discoveries are made, our understanding of this remarkable monument will continue to grow, offering new insights into the lives and beliefs of our prehistoric ancestors.

The mystery and majesty of Stonehenge ensure that it will remain an enduring subject of fascination and study for generations to come. Its stones stand as silent witnesses to the passage of millennia, inviting us to ponder the ingenuity and spirituality of the ancient people who created this extraordinary testament to human endeavor and imagination.

Chapter 3: Parthenon

The Parthenon, an enduring symbol of ancient Greece and one of the most iconic structures in the world, stands majestically atop the Acropolis in Athens. Constructed between 447 and 432 BC during the height of the Athenian Empire, it was dedicated to the goddess Athena, the city's patron deity, and represents the pinnacle of classical Greek architecture. The Parthenon epitomizes the artistic and architectural innovations of its time and serves as a testament to the cultural and political achievements of Athens during its Golden Age.

The construction of the Parthenon was part of a grand building program initiated by the Athenian statesman Pericles, who sought to demonstrate the glory and power of Athens following the Persian Wars. Designed by the architects Ictinus and Callicrates, with significant contributions from the sculptor Phidias, the Parthenon was built to replace an earlier temple destroyed by the Persians in 480 BC. The new temple not only honored Athena but also celebrated the Athenian victory over the Persians and the democratic ideals of the city-state.

The Parthenon's architectural design exemplifies the Doric order, the simplest and sturdiest of the classical orders, characterized by its fluted columns, plain capitals, and triglyph-metope frieze. However, the Parthenon incorporates elements of the Ionic order, such as the continuous frieze that runs along the inner colonnade of the cella, or inner chamber. This blend of Doric and Ionic features reflects the innovative spirit of the architects and the desire to create a unique and harmonious structure.

The dimensions of the Parthenon are remarkable for their precision and symmetry. The temple measures 69.5 meters (228 feet) in length, 30.9 meters (101 feet) in width, and 13.72 meters (45 feet) in height. It originally consisted of 46 outer columns and 19 inner columns, each standing 10.4 meters (34 feet) high and 1.9 meters (6.2 feet) in diameter at the base. The columns exhibit entasis, a slight curvature that corrects the optical illusion of concavity that occurs when viewing straight lines from a distance. This subtle adjustment enhances the overall aesthetic harmony and balance of the structure.

The Parthenon's sculptural decoration, overseen by Phidias, is renowned for its artistic excellence and intricate detail. The most famous sculptures include the metopes, the frieze, and the pediments. The metopes, 92 in total, depict scenes of mythological battles such as the Gigantomachy (battle between gods and giants), the Centauromachy (battle between Lapiths and centaurs), and the Amazonomachy (battle between Greeks and Amazons). These dynamic and dramatic scenes symbolize the triumph of order over chaos and civilization over barbarism.

The continuous frieze, measuring 160 meters (524 feet) in length, is one of the most celebrated aspects of the Parthenon's decoration. It portrays the Panathenaic Procession, a religious festival held in honor of Athena every four years. The frieze depicts various groups of Athenians, including horsemen, musicians, and priests, along with scenes of sacrificial animals and deities observing the procession. The inclusion of ordinary citizens in the frieze is a testament to the democratic values of Athens, emphasizing the unity and participation of its people in civic and religious life.

The pediments, the triangular gables at either end of the Parthenon, are adorned with large sculptural groups that illustrate significant mythological events. The east pediment depicts the birth of Athena from the head of Zeus, surrounded by other gods and goddesses. The west pediment shows the contest between Athena and Poseidon for the patronage of Athens, with Athena emerging victorious by offering the olive tree, a symbol of peace and prosperity. These sculptural compositions are masterful in their use of space and movement, creating a vivid and dramatic narrative.

The centerpiece of the Parthenon was the colossal statue of Athena Parthenos, crafted by Phidias and housed within the cella. Made of gold and ivory (chryselephantine), the statue stood approximately 12 meters (39 feet) tall and depicted Athena holding a smaller statue of Nike, the goddess of victory, in her right hand, while her left hand rested on a shield. Athena was adorned with a helmet, a spear, and an aegis featuring the head of Medusa. This statue was not only a religious icon but also a symbol of the wealth and artistic prowess of Athens. Unfortunately, the original statue was lost in antiquity, but descriptions and later copies provide an idea of its grandeur.

The Parthenon's construction involved advanced engineering techniques and meticulous craftsmanship. The blocks of marble used in its construction were quarried from Mount Pentelicus, about 16 kilometers (10 miles) northeast of Athens. These blocks were precisely cut and fitted together without the use of mortar, relying instead on the precise interlocking of the stone and metal clamps to hold them in place. The transportation and assembly of these massive stones required sophisticated planning and coordination, reflecting the high level of skill and organization of the ancient Athenian builders.

The Parthenon has undergone significant changes throughout its history. During the early Christian period, it was converted into a church dedicated to the Virgin Mary, and many of the original sculptures were removed or altered. Following the Ottoman conquest of Greece in the 15th century, the Parthenon was transformed into a mosque, complete with a minaret. In 1687, during the Venetian siege of Athens, the Parthenon suffered severe damage when an Ottoman ammunition dump stored inside the building exploded, causing extensive destruction to the structure and its sculptures.

In the early 19th century, the British ambassador to the Ottoman Empire, Lord Elgin, obtained permission to remove a significant portion of the surviving sculptures, which were later transported to England and became known as the Elgin Marbles. These sculptures are now housed in the British Museum, and their removal has been a subject of ongoing controversy and calls for repatriation by the Greek government. Efforts to preserve and restore the Parthenon began in the 19th century and continue to this day. Modern conservation projects aim to stabilize the structure, repair damage caused by pollution and previous restorations, and protect the monument from further deterioration. These efforts are guided by principles of minimal intervention and the use of materials and techniques compatible with the original construction.

The Parthenon stands not only as a marvel of ancient engineering and artistry but also as a symbol of the enduring legacy of classical Greek culture. It represents the ideals of beauty, harmony, and proportion that have influenced Western art and architecture for centuries. The principles of Greek architecture, as exemplified by the Parthenon, laid the foundation for the development of Roman architecture and, by extension, the architectural traditions of the Renaissance and modern Western society.

The cultural and historical significance of the Parthenon extends beyond its architectural achievements. It is a powerful symbol of the political and intellectual achievements of ancient Athens, a city that produced remarkable advancements in philosophy, science, drama, and democracy. Figures such as Socrates, Plato, Aristotle, and Pericles contributed to a cultural flourishing that has profoundly shaped Western civilization.

In addition to its historical and cultural importance, the Parthenon continues to be a focal point for discussions about heritage, preservation, and the role of ancient monuments in contemporary society. It serves as a reminder of the complexities of cultural ownership and the importance of preserving our shared human heritage for future generations. The ongoing debate over the return of the Elgin Marbles highlights broader issues related to the repatriation of cultural artifacts and the responsibilities of museums and institutions in preserving and interpreting the past.

Today, the Parthenon remains a symbol of national pride for Greece and a source of inspiration for people around the world. Visitors to the Acropolis can experience the awe-inspiring beauty and grandeur of this ancient temple, gaining a deeper appreciation for the achievements of the ancient Greeks and the enduring legacy of their civilization. The Parthenon stands as a testament to the human capacity for creativity, innovation, and the pursuit of excellence, embodying values that continue to resonate across time and cultures.

Chapter 4: Colosseum

The Colosseum, also known as the Flavian Amphitheater, is one of the most iconic symbols of ancient Rome and a masterpiece of engineering and architecture. Located in the heart of Rome, Italy, this colossal structure was commissioned by Emperor Vespasian of the Flavian dynasty in AD 70-72 and completed in AD 80 under his successor and heir, Titus. Further modifications were made during the reign of Vespasian's younger son, Domitian. The Colosseum's construction was a monumental endeavor, involving thousands of laborers, including slaves and skilled artisans, who worked tirelessly to bring this ambitious project to life. It stands as a testament to the power, ingenuity, and grandeur of the Roman Empire.

The Colosseum was built to host a variety of public spectacles, the most famous of which were gladiatorial contests. These brutal events, where gladiators—often slaves, prisoners of war, or condemned criminals—fought to the death for the entertainment of the masses, were a central aspect of Roman culture and society. Additionally, the Colosseum hosted animal hunts, executions, re-enactments of famous battles, and dramas based on classical mythology. These spectacles were part of the "bread and circuses" strategy employed by Roman emperors to appease and distract the populace from political issues and maintain public order.

The Colosseum's architectural design is a marvel of engineering. The elliptical structure measures 189 meters (620 feet) long, 156 meters (512 feet) wide, and 50 meters (164 feet) high, with a perimeter of 545 meters (1,788 feet). It could accommodate between 50,000 and 80,000 spectators, who were seated according to their social status. The seating arrangement reflected the rigid hierarchical nature of Roman society, with the best seats reserved for the emperor, senators, and other elite members of society, while the common people sat in the upper tiers.

The exterior of the Colosseum features three levels of arches topped by a fourth level adorned with pilasters. Each of the three levels comprises 80 arches, which not only provided structural support but also allowed for efficient crowd movement. The arches on the first three levels are framed by semi-engaged columns in the Doric, Ionic, and Corinthian orders, respectively, showcasing the Romans' mastery of classical architectural styles. The fourth level, known as the attic, was originally decorated with Corinthian pilasters and had small rectangular windows. This level also featured a series of bronze shields and painted stucco reliefs, adding to the grandeur of the façade.

One of the most impressive features of the Colosseum is its complex system of vaults and corridors. The use of concrete and the barrel vault, a structural innovation of the Romans, allowed for the construction of the immense interior space without the need for columns to support the weight. This system of vaults and corridors not only supported the seating areas but also facilitated the efficient movement of spectators, performers, and animals. The hypogeum, an underground network of tunnels and chambers beneath the arena floor, housed the gladiators, animals, and machinery used to stage the spectacles. Elevators and pulleys were used to lift the animals and gladiators to the arena floor, adding an element of surprise and excitement to the events.

The arena floor itself was made of wood and covered with sand, which could be quickly cleaned or replaced after the bloody contests. The Latin word for sand, "harena," is the origin of the word "arena." The arena was equipped with numerous trapdoors and lifts, allowing for dramatic entrances and exits. The floor could also be flooded to stage mock naval battles, known as naumachiae, demonstrating the versatility and ingenuity of Roman engineering.

The Colosseum's inauguration was a grand affair that lasted for 100 days, during which thousands of gladiators and animals were killed. These inaugural games set the standard for the spectacles that would follow and solidified the Colosseum's status as the premier venue for public entertainment in the Roman Empire. Over the centuries, the Colosseum witnessed countless events, from gladiatorial combats to public executions, and became a symbol of the might and sophistication of Roman civilization.

Despite its grandeur, the Colosseum's history is also marked by periods of neglect and destruction. Following the decline of the Roman Empire, the Colosseum fell into disrepair. It suffered damage from earthquakes, and many of its stones were repurposed for other building projects in Rome. During the medieval period, the Colosseum was used as a fortress and later as a quarry, with much of its valuable travertine stone removed. It was not until the 18th and 19th centuries that efforts were made to preserve and restore the Colosseum as a historical monument.

Today, the Colosseum stands as a powerful symbol of ancient Rome and attracts millions of visitors each year. It has been recognized as a UNESCO World Heritage site and is considered one of the New Seven Wonders of the World. The ongoing conservation efforts aim to stabilize the structure and protect it from further damage caused by pollution, weathering, and the sheer number of tourists.

The Colosseum's cultural and historical significance extends beyond its architectural and engineering achievements. It serves as a reminder of the complexities and contradictions of Roman society, where grand displays of power and wealth coexisted with brutal spectacles of violence and death. The gladiatorial games, in particular, highlight the Roman obsession with martial prowess and the glorification of violence as a means of demonstrating imperial strength.

In addition to its role as an entertainment venue, the Colosseum has also been a site of political and social significance. Throughout its history, it has been used to host ceremonies, public gatherings, and political events. In modern times, the Colosseum has become a symbol of resistance and human rights. It has been illuminated in gold to protest the death penalty and in red to commemorate the victims of religious persecution, demonstrating its continued relevance as a symbol of both historical memory and contemporary values.

The Colosseum's influence on architecture and design is also profound. Its innovative use of concrete and arches laid the foundation for future architectural developments in the Roman Empire and beyond. The amphitheater's design has inspired countless arenas and stadiums around the world, from ancient times to the present day. The principles of Roman engineering, as exemplified by the Colosseum, continue to inform modern construction techniques and urban planning.

The study of the Colosseum provides valuable insights into the social, cultural, and political dynamics of ancient Rome. Archaeological research, including excavations and advanced imaging techniques, has revealed new information about the construction methods, the lives of the people who built and used the Colosseum, and the broader context of Roman society. These discoveries enrich our understanding of the ancient world and underscore the importance of preserving our cultural heritage for future generations.

The Colosseum remains a powerful symbol of the enduring legacy of the Roman Empire. Its imposing presence and rich history continue to captivate the imagination of people around the world. As we walk through its ancient corridors and stand in the shadow of its towering arches, we are reminded of the remarkable achievements of Roman engineering and architecture, as well as the complex and often brutal nature of Roman society. The Colosseum stands as a testament to the ingenuity and resilience of the human spirit, a symbol of both the grandeur and the contradictions of our shared past.

Chapter 5: Machu Picchu

Machu Picchu, often referred to as the "Lost City of the Incas," is one of the most iconic and enigmatic archaeological sites in the world. Nestled high in the Andes Mountains of Peru, at an elevation of approximately 2,430 meters (7,970 feet), this ancient citadel represents the pinnacle of Inca engineering and architecture. Built in the 15th century during the reign of the Inca emperor Pachacuti, Machu Picchu is a testament to the ingenuity, resilience, and cultural achievements of the Inca civilization.

The exact purpose of Machu Picchu remains a subject of scholarly debate, but it is widely believed to have been a royal estate or a religious retreat for the Inca elite. The site was abandoned in the 16th century during the Spanish conquest and remained largely unknown to the outside world until its rediscovery by American historian Hiram Bingham in 1911. Since then, Machu Picchu has become a symbol of Inca heritage and a UNESCO World Heritage site, attracting millions of visitors each year.

The journey to Machu Picchu itself is an awe-inspiring experience, with visitors often traveling by train from the city of Cusco to the town of Aguas Calientes, followed by a bus ride up the winding roads to the entrance of the site. For those seeking a more immersive experience, the Inca Trail, a multi-day trek through the Andes, offers breathtaking views and a chance to follow in the footsteps of the ancient Incas. The trail passes through diverse landscapes, including lush cloud forests, alpine tundra, and stunning mountain passes, providing a sense of the natural beauty and isolation that characterized Machu Picchu.

Upon arrival, the first glimpse of Machu Picchu is nothing short of breathtaking. The site is divided into two main areas: the agricultural sector and the urban sector. The agricultural terraces, which cascade down the mountainside, are a marvel of ancient engineering. These terraces not only provided arable land for farming but also helped prevent soil erosion and managed water drainage in the steep terrain. The terraces are supported by stone retaining walls and were likely used to grow crops such as maize, potatoes, and quinoa, which were staples of the Inca diet.

The urban sector is a labyrinth of stone buildings, plazas, temples, and other structures, all constructed using the Inca technique of dry-stone masonry. This method involves fitting stones together without the use of mortar, relying on precise cutting and placement to ensure stability and durability. The skill of Inca stonemasons is evident in the tight joints and the way the structures have withstood centuries of earthquakes and weathering.

One of the most significant and impressive structures within Machu Picchu is the Temple of the Sun, also known as the Torreón. This semi-circular building, constructed around a large rock, features finely crafted stonework and a series of trapezoidal windows that align with the solstices, allowing sunlight to illuminate the interior during important astronomical events. The Temple of the Sun likely served as an observatory and a place of worship dedicated to Inti, the sun god, who was one of the most important deities in the Inca pantheon.

Adjacent to the Temple of the Sun is the Royal Tomb, a finely carved cave that may have been used for ceremonial purposes or as a burial site for important individuals. The intricate stonework and the presence of niches and carved steps suggest that this was a significant and sacred space.

Another notable structure is the Intihuatana Stone, often referred to as the "Hitching Post of the Sun." This carved stone pillar, situated on a raised platform, is believed to have been used as an astronomical clock or calendar. The Intihuatana Stone aligns with key astronomical events, such as the equinoxes and solstices, and may have been used to track the movements of the sun and other celestial bodies. The name "Intihuatana" means "place to tie up the sun" in Quechua, reflecting the stone's importance in Inca cosmology and its role in rituals intended to ensure the sun's return.

The Sacred Plaza, located near the center of Machu Picchu, is surrounded by some of the site's most important buildings, including the Temple of the Three Windows and the Principal Temple. The Temple of the Three Windows features three large trapezoidal windows that frame stunning views of the surrounding mountains. The Principal Temple, characterized by its finely cut stone walls and large size, was likely a major ceremonial site. Both structures reflect the Inca emphasis on astronomical alignment, religious significance, and architectural prowess.

The residential sector of Machu Picchu includes a variety of buildings, ranging from simple one-room structures to more elaborate multi-room houses. These buildings were constructed using the same dry-stone masonry techniques and were likely used to house the site's inhabitants, who would have included priests, nobles, and workers. The presence of finely crafted stonework and the overall layout of the residential sector suggest a high level of organization and planning.

One of the most intriguing aspects of Machu Picchu is its advanced water management system. The site features a series of fountains, channels, and drainage systems that efficiently managed the flow of water throughout the complex. The Inca engineers designed these systems to take advantage of the natural springs and rainfall, ensuring a reliable water supply for drinking, irrigation, and ceremonial purposes. The main water source, known as the Spring of the Inca, is located near the site's entrance and feeds a series of interconnected fountains and channels that distribute water to various parts of the complex.

The architectural and engineering achievements of Machu Picchu are complemented by its stunning natural setting. The site is surrounded by towering peaks, lush green valleys, and the winding Urubamba River below. The dramatic landscape adds to the sense of mystery and awe that Machu Picchu inspires, and it is easy to understand why the Incas chose this remote and beautiful location for such an important site. The strategic location of Machu Picchu also provided a natural defense against potential invaders, further underscoring the ingenuity of Inca planning.

Despite its remote location, Machu Picchu was connected to the wider Inca Empire through a network of roads and trails, known as the Qhapaq Ñan or Inca Road System. This extensive network facilitated communication, trade, and the movement of armies across the diverse and challenging terrain of the Andes. The Inca Trail, one of the most famous segments of this network, provides a direct link between Machu Picchu and the Inca capital of Cusco, highlighting the strategic importance of the site within the empire.

The rediscovery of Machu Picchu in 1911 by Hiram Bingham brought global attention to this remarkable site and sparked a renewed interest in Inca history and culture. Bingham's expeditions, sponsored by Yale University and the National Geographic Society, resulted in extensive documentation, excavation, and the removal of many artifacts, which were taken to the United States. This removal of artifacts has been a source of controversy, with ongoing debates and negotiations between Peru and Yale University regarding the repatriation of these cultural treasures.

Since its rediscovery, Machu Picchu has been the focus of extensive archaeological research, conservation efforts, and tourism development. Scholars have studied the site to gain a deeper understanding of Inca society, architecture, and engineering, while conservationists have worked to preserve the fragile structures and protect the site from the impacts of tourism and environmental degradation. In 1983, Machu Picchu was designated a UNESCO World Heritage site, recognizing its outstanding universal value and the need for ongoing protection.

Tourism at Machu Picchu has grown significantly over the past few decades, with hundreds of thousands of visitors arriving each year to experience the wonder of this ancient citadel. While tourism provides important economic benefits for the local communities and the Peruvian economy, it also presents significant challenges for the preservation of the site. The impact of foot traffic, erosion, and infrastructure development has raised concerns about the long-term sustainability of tourism at Machu Picchu.

In response to these challenges, the Peruvian government and various international organizations have implemented measures to manage and mitigate the impacts of tourism. These measures include limiting the number of daily visitors, creating designated pathways to control foot traffic, and promoting responsible tourism practices. Additionally, efforts are underway to develop sustainable tourism initiatives that benefit local communities while preserving the cultural and natural heritage of Machu Picchu.

Machu Picchu's significance extends beyond its historical and architectural achievements. It serves as a powerful symbol of Inca culture and heritage, representing the ingenuity, resilience, and spiritual beliefs of this remarkable civilization. The site continues to inspire wonder and admiration, offering a glimpse into a world that existed long before the arrival of Europeans in the Americas.

For many visitors, a trip to Machu Picchu is a deeply moving and transformative experience. The combination of breathtaking natural beauty, awe-inspiring architecture, and the palpable sense of history creates a profound connection to the past. The site stands as a testament to the enduring legacy of the Inca civilization and the human capacity for creativity, innovation, and reverence for the natural world.

Chapter 6: Petra

Petra, an archaeological wonder nestled in the rugged mountains of southern Jordan, is a testament to the ingenuity and creativity of the Nabataean civilization. Known as the "Rose City" due to the reddish hue of its rock-cut architecture, Petra was the capital of the Nabataean Kingdom from the 4th century BCE to the 2nd century CE. This ancient city is renowned for its stunning facades carved directly into the cliffs, intricate tombs, temples, and advanced water management systems, making it one of the most remarkable historical sites in the world.

The origins of Petra can be traced back to the nomadic Nabataeans, an Arab tribe that settled in the region and established a prosperous trade network. The strategic location of Petra, at the crossroads of major trade routes linking the Arabian Peninsula, Egypt, and the Mediterranean, allowed the Nabataeans to control and benefit from the lucrative spice and incense trade. This economic prosperity enabled them to develop a sophisticated urban center, characterized by its unique blend of Eastern and Hellenistic architectural styles.

The entrance to Petra is through the Siq, a narrow gorge approximately 1.2 kilometers (0.75 miles) long, flanked by towering cliffs that rise up to 80 meters (262 feet) high. The dramatic approach through the Siq, with its winding path and occasional glimpses of the sky above, creates a sense of anticipation and awe. The Siq itself is a geological marvel, formed by natural processes over millions of years. Along its walls, visitors can see remnants of ancient carvings and niches that once held religious icons, as well as a sophisticated water conduit system that supplied the city with fresh water.

Emerging from the Siq, visitors are greeted by the breathtaking sight of Al-Khazneh, commonly known as the Treasury. This iconic structure, with its ornate façade carved directly into the sandstone cliff, is one of the most famous and well-preserved monuments in Petra.

Standing at 39.1 meters (128 feet) high and 25.4 meters (83 feet) wide, the Treasury features a blend of Nabataean and Greco-Roman architectural elements, including columns, friezes, and statues. While its exact purpose remains a mystery, it is believed to have been a royal tomb or a temple dedicated to the Nabataean gods.

Beyond the Treasury lies the heart of Petra, a sprawling cityscape filled with a multitude of tombs, temples, and public buildings. The Street of Facades, lined with tombs carved into the cliffs, leads to the Theatre, a grand structure capable of seating up to 8,500 spectators. The Theatre, carved directly into the rock, reflects the influence of Hellenistic architecture and showcases the Nabataeans' ability to adapt and incorporate elements from other cultures.

One of the most significant structures in Petra is the Monastery, or Ad-Deir, which rivals the Treasury in its grandeur and scale. Located on a high plateau accessible by climbing over 800 rock-cut steps, the Monastery stands at 47 meters (154 feet) wide and 48.3 meters (158 feet) high. Its façade, featuring large columns and a central doorway, is less ornate than the Treasury but equally impressive. The Monastery is believed to have served as a religious center and possibly a site for pilgrimage, reflecting the Nabataeans' spiritual and cultural life.

The Great Temple, another prominent structure in Petra, is a massive complex that once served as the city's primary place of worship. Covering an area of over 7,560 square meters (81,400 square feet), the temple complex includes a large colonnaded courtyard, a grand staircase, and several chambers and sanctuaries. The architectural features of the Great Temple, including its Corinthian columns and intricate carvings, highlight the fusion of Nabataean and Greco-Roman influences.

Petra's advanced water management system is a testament to the ingenuity and engineering prowess of the Nabataeans. Despite the arid environment, the Nabataeans developed an extensive network of dams, cisterns, and aqueducts to collect, store, and distribute water throughout the city. This system ensured a reliable water supply for drinking, agriculture, and religious rituals, and played a crucial role in sustaining the city's population and supporting its prosperity. The importance of water in Petra is also evident in the numerous public fountains and baths that once adorned the city.

The Royal Tombs, a series of monumental tombs carved into the cliffs overlooking the city center, provide further insight into the Nabataean burial practices and architectural achievements. These tombs, including the Urn Tomb, the Silk Tomb, the Corinthian Tomb, and the Palace Tomb, are characterized by their elaborate facades and intricate carvings. The Urn Tomb, for example, features a large courtyard, a central hall, and several smaller chambers, reflecting the social and political status of the individuals buried within.

In addition to its architectural and engineering marvels, Petra was also a vibrant cultural and commercial hub. The city hosted a diverse population, including Nabataeans, Greeks, Romans, and other traders and travelers from across the ancient world. This cultural melting pot is reflected in the eclectic mix of artistic and architectural styles found throughout the city. Petra's marketplace, or souq, was a bustling center of trade, where merchants sold goods such as spices, textiles, and precious metals. The presence of caravanserais, or inns, provided accommodation for travelers and facilitated the exchange of ideas and goods.

Petra's decline began in the 2nd century CE, following the Roman annexation of the Nabataean Kingdom. The city's importance as a trade hub diminished as new trade routes emerged, and it eventually fell into obscurity. A series of earthquakes in the 4th and 6th centuries further contributed to the city's decline, leading to the abandonment of many of its structures. By the 7th century, Petra was largely deserted, and its existence faded from historical records.

The rediscovery of Petra in 1812 by Swiss explorer Johann Ludwig Burckhardt brought the city back to the world's attention. Burckhardt, disguised as a Muslim pilgrim, managed to gain access to the site and documented his findings, sparking interest among European scholars and explorers. Subsequent archaeological expeditions in the 19th and 20th centuries uncovered more of Petra's secrets, revealing its historical and cultural significance.

Today, Petra is a UNESCO World Heritage site and one of the most popular tourist destinations in the Middle East. The site attracts visitors from around the world who come to marvel at its stunning architecture, explore its ancient ruins, and learn about the rich history of the Nabataean civilization. Despite the challenges posed by tourism and environmental factors, efforts are underway to preserve and protect Petra's unique heritage for future generations.

The cultural and historical significance of Petra extends beyond its physical remains. The city serves as a symbol of the enduring legacy of the Nabataean people, their adaptability, and their contributions to the ancient world. Petra's architecture and engineering innovations continue to inspire and inform modern scholars and architects, while its art and cultural artifacts provide valuable insights into the lives and beliefs of the Nabataeans.

Petra's allure also lies in its ability to evoke a sense of mystery and wonder. The city's remote location, hidden within the mountains, and its intricate rock-cut architecture create an atmosphere of enchantment and intrigue. The experience of exploring Petra, from the narrow Siq to the majestic Treasury and beyond, allows visitors to step back in time and immerse themselves in the ancient world.

In addition to its historical and archaeological significance, Petra holds a special place in the cultural consciousness of Jordan and the wider Arab world. It is a source of national pride and identity, celebrated for its beauty, resilience, and cultural heritage. The site is also a symbol of the broader cultural and historical connections between the Arab world and the ancient civilizations that once thrived in the region.

The future of Petra depends on the continued efforts to balance tourism, preservation, and sustainability. Initiatives to manage visitor numbers, protect the site's fragile structures, and engage local communities in conservation efforts are crucial for ensuring that Petra remains a vibrant and accessible destination for generations to come. Collaborative efforts between the Jordanian government, international organizations, and local stakeholders are essential for safeguarding Petra's heritage and promoting sustainable tourism practices.

Chapter 7: Angkor Wat

Angkor Wat, located in the dense jungles of Cambodia, stands as a monument to the grandeur and spiritual ambition of the Khmer Empire. Built in the early 12th century by King Suryavarman II, this architectural marvel is the largest religious monument in the world, covering an area of 162.6 hectares (1.6 million square meters). Initially dedicated to the Hindu god Vishnu, Angkor Wat later transformed into a Buddhist temple, reflecting the religious shifts that occurred within the Khmer Empire over the centuries.

The construction of Angkor Wat began in the early 12th century and is believed to have taken around 30 years to complete. The temple's primary purpose was to serve as both a state temple and a mausoleum for King Suryavarman II. The choice to dedicate the temple to Vishnu, rather than the traditional deity Shiva, signifies a significant religious and cultural shift. This dedication was intended to legitimize Suryavarman II's rule and solidify his divine right to govern.

One of the most remarkable aspects of Angkor Wat is its architectural design, which embodies the classical style of Khmer architecture. The temple is oriented to the west, unlike most Angkorian temples, which face east. This orientation has led to various interpretations, with some scholars suggesting that it aligns with funerary traditions, while others believe it may be linked to Vishnu's association with the west. The temple's layout is a representation of Mount Meru, the home of the gods in Hindu mythology. The central tower, standing at 65 meters (213 feet) high, symbolizes the sacred mountain's peak, while the surrounding towers and enclosures represent the lower ranges and the universe's concentric seas.

The temple complex is surrounded by a vast moat, measuring 1.5 kilometers (0.93 miles) by 1.3 kilometers (0.81 miles), and a high outer wall. This moat not only provided a defensive barrier but also symbolized the oceans surrounding Mount Meru. Visitors enter the temple via a long causeway, flanked by naga balustrades, which are intricately carved stone serpents that serve both a decorative and symbolic purpose. The naga, or serpent deity, is an important figure in Hindu and Buddhist mythology, representing fertility, protection, and the bridge between heaven and earth.

The main entrance to Angkor Wat is through the western gate, a massive stone structure adorned with intricate carvings and bas-reliefs. These carvings depict various scenes from Hindu epics such as the Ramayana and the Mahabharata, as well as historical events and celestial beings. The attention to detail and the high level of craftsmanship evident in these bas-reliefs highlight the artistic and cultural achievements of the Khmer Empire.

Inside the temple complex, visitors are greeted by a series of galleries and courtyards, each more impressive than the last. The outer gallery, known as the Hall of the Thousand Buddhas, once contained numerous statues of Buddha, many of which have been lost or removed over the centuries. The walls of this gallery are adorned with bas-reliefs depicting scenes from Hindu mythology, historical battles, and daily life in the Khmer Empire. These bas-reliefs are not only artistic masterpieces but also provide valuable insights into the religious, social, and political life of the period.

One of the most famous bas-reliefs in Angkor Wat is the Churning of the Ocean of Milk, located in the eastern gallery. This intricate carving depicts a central event in Hindu mythology, where gods (Devas) and demons (Asuras) cooperate to churn the ocean in order to obtain Amrita, the elixir of immortality. The scene is filled with dynamic figures, each contributing to the massive effort, and the attention to detail in their expressions and movements is remarkable. This bas-relief exemplifies the Khmer Empire's artistic sophistication and their deep connection to Hindu mythology.

The central sanctuary, or quincunx, is the heart of Angkor Wat and represents the cosmic axis, connecting the human world to the divine. This area consists of a series of rising terraces, each smaller than the last, culminating in the central tower. The central tower houses the main shrine, originally dedicated to Vishnu and later converted to house Buddhist relics. The ascent to the central sanctuary is steep, symbolizing the arduous journey to spiritual enlightenment and the effort required to reach the divine.

The architectural techniques used in constructing Angkor Wat are equally impressive. The temple was built using sandstone blocks, which were transported from the Kulen Mountains, located over 50 kilometers (31 miles) away. The precise methods used to transport these massive stones remain a topic of scholarly debate, but it is believed that a combination of waterways and labor-intensive techniques were employed. The stones were meticulously cut and fitted together without the use of mortar, a testament to the skill and precision of Khmer craftsmen.

Angkor Wat's construction also involved an advanced understanding of astronomy and cosmology. The temple's layout and orientation are aligned with celestial events, such as the equinoxes and solstices. The central tower is said to align with the morning sun on the spring equinox, symbolizing the union of heaven and earth. This alignment underscores the Khmer Empire's sophisticated knowledge of astronomy and their desire to reflect cosmic order in their architectural endeavors.

The transformation of Angkor Wat from a Hindu temple to a Buddhist site began in the late 13th century, following the decline of Hinduism and the rise of Theravada Buddhism in the region. This religious transition did not result in significant structural changes to the temple but led to the addition of Buddhist statues, paintings, and inscriptions. Angkor Wat became an important pilgrimage site for Buddhists, further cementing its status as a spiritual and cultural landmark.

The decline of the Khmer Empire in the 15th century led to the gradual abandonment of Angkor Wat. The reasons for this decline are complex and multifaceted, including factors such as political instability, environmental changes, and shifts in trade routes. Despite its abandonment, Angkor Wat remained relatively intact, largely due to its continuous use as a Buddhist temple and the protection offered by the surrounding jungle.

The rediscovery of Angkor Wat by Western explorers in the 19th century brought the temple to international attention. French explorer Henri Mouhot's detailed descriptions and sketches of the site in 1860 captured the imagination of the world and sparked a renewed interest in the history and culture of the Khmer Empire. Subsequent archaeological studies and restoration efforts have uncovered much of Angkor Wat's history and ensured its preservation for future generations.

Today, Angkor Wat is a UNESCO World Heritage site and a symbol of Cambodia's rich cultural heritage. The temple complex attracts millions of visitors each year, drawn by its breathtaking architecture, historical significance, and spiritual atmosphere. Tourism has become a vital part of the local economy, providing much-needed revenue and employment opportunities. However, the influx of visitors also poses challenges to the preservation of the site, necessitating careful management and conservation efforts.

Efforts to protect and conserve Angkor Wat are spearheaded by various organizations, including the Cambodian government, UNESCO, and international conservation groups. These efforts include measures to control visitor access, restore damaged structures, and address environmental threats such as water damage and vegetation overgrowth. Advanced technologies, such as laser scanning and digital mapping, are used to document and analyze the site, aiding in the development of effective conservation strategies.

The cultural and spiritual significance of Angkor Wat extends beyond its physical structure. The temple is a source of national pride for Cambodians and a symbol of their historical resilience and creativity. It serves as a reminder of the Khmer Empire's contributions to art, architecture, and religion, and its enduring influence on Southeast Asian culture. Angkor Wat's iconic silhouette, featuring its soaring towers and intricate carvings, has become a symbol of Cambodia itself, appearing on the national flag and currency.

Angkor Wat's influence can also be seen in the broader context of Southeast Asian art and architecture. The temple's design and decorative elements have inspired countless other structures in the region, from temples in Thailand and Laos to religious monuments in Vietnam and Indonesia. The spread of Khmer architectural styles and techniques reflects the historical interconnectedness of Southeast Asian cultures and the shared artistic heritage that continues to shape the region's identity.

Chapter 8: The Great Wall of China

The Great Wall of China, often lauded as one of the most remarkable architectural feats in human history, stretches across the northern expanse of China, weaving its way through mountains, deserts, and plains. Its construction spanned several dynasties and thousands of years, creating a structure that not only served as a formidable defensive barrier but also symbolized the unity and enduring spirit of the Chinese people. The wall's length is estimated at about 13,170 miles (21,196 kilometers), including its branches, making it the longest man-made structure in the world. The Great Wall is not a single, continuous wall but a series of walls and fortifications built at different times, reflecting the changing needs and capabilities of the Chinese states and dynasties.

The origins of the Great Wall can be traced back to the 7th century BCE during the Warring States period. During this time, various states built walls to defend their territories from rival states and nomadic invaders. The state of Chu is credited with constructing the first sections of the wall, followed by other states such as Qi, Yan, and Zhao. These early walls were made of rammed earth and wood, utilizing the natural terrain to enhance their defensive capabilities. The fragmented nature of these early walls meant that they were primarily local defenses rather than a unified structure.

The unification of China under the Qin Dynasty in 221 BCE marked a significant turning point in the history of the Great Wall. Emperor Qin Shi Huang, the first emperor of China, initiated the construction of a unified wall to protect the newly unified empire from the Xiongnu, nomadic tribes from the north. This ambitious project involved connecting and extending the existing walls built by previous states. The construction of the Qin Wall required the mobilization of hundreds of thousands of laborers, including soldiers, peasants, and prisoners. The work was grueling and dangerous, often leading to harsh conditions and high mortality rates among the laborers.

The Qin Wall, made primarily of rammed earth, extended from the eastern part of China in the Bohai Sea to the western region of Gansu Province. This wall laid the foundation for future expansions and improvements during subsequent dynasties. Despite its impressive scale, the Qin Wall was relatively rudimentary compared to later constructions, and it required constant maintenance and reinforcement to remain effective against invasions.

Following the fall of the Qin Dynasty, the Han Dynasty (206 BCE – 220 CE) continued to build and expand the Great Wall. The Han emperors extended the wall further west to protect the Silk Road trade routes, which were vital for the economic prosperity of the empire. The Han Wall incorporated watchtowers, beacon towers, and garrison stations to improve communication and coordination along the wall. These structures allowed the Han military to quickly respond to threats and mobilize troops where needed. The Han Wall also featured more sophisticated construction techniques, such as the use of bricks and stones in some sections, providing greater durability and strength.

The Great Wall saw further development during the Northern Wei, Northern Qi, and Sui Dynasties, each contributing to its expansion and fortification. However, it was during the Ming Dynasty (1368-1644) that the Great Wall took on the form that is most familiar to us today. The Ming emperors faced constant threats from the Mongols and other nomadic groups, prompting a massive reconstruction and expansion of the wall. The Ming Wall was built using more advanced materials and techniques, including bricks, stones, and mortar, making it much more durable and imposing than previous versions.

The Ming Wall extended from Jiayu Pass in the west to Shanhaiguan in the east, with numerous branches and spurs connecting strategic locations. The wall's design incorporated a series of defensive features, including watchtowers, beacon towers, and fortresses, which allowed for better surveillance, communication, and defense. The watchtowers, typically spaced at regular intervals along the wall, provided vantage points for spotting enemy movements and signaling to other towers using smoke signals during the day and fire signals at night. These towers were also used as barracks, storerooms, and armories, housing soldiers and supplies necessary for the wall's defense.

One of the most famous sections of the Ming Wall is the Badaling section, located near Beijing. This section, known for its impressive architecture and stunning scenery, has been extensively restored and is a popular tourist destination. The Badaling section features wide ramparts that allowed for the movement of troops and horses, as well as crenellated parapets for archers to shoot from cover. The strategic importance of this section is underscored by its proximity to Beijing, the capital of the Ming Dynasty, and its role in protecting the political and cultural heart of China.

Another notable section of the Ming Wall is the Jinshanling section, known for its steep climbs and well-preserved watchtowers. This section provides a glimpse into the military strategy and architectural ingenuity of the Ming builders. The Jinshanling section, with its complex system of walls, towers, and fortifications, showcases the defensive depth and resilience of the Great Wall. The rugged terrain and challenging construction conditions highlight the extraordinary effort and dedication required to build and maintain the wall.

Despite its formidable appearance, the Great Wall was not an impenetrable barrier. Throughout its history, various nomadic groups, including the Mongols under Genghis Khan and later under Kublai Khan, managed to breach the wall and invade China. The wall's effectiveness depended on the strength and vigilance of the garrisoned troops, as well as the ability of the central government to maintain and support its defenses. The Great Wall served as a deterrent and a delaying tactic, providing time for the Chinese military to mobilize and respond to threats.

The significance of the Great Wall extends beyond its military function. It served as a symbol of the unity and determination of the Chinese people to protect their homeland. The wall also facilitated trade and cultural exchanges between China and neighboring regions, contributing to the development of the Silk Road and the spread of ideas, technologies, and goods. The Great Wall played a role in defining the cultural and geographical boundaries of China, shaping the nation's identity and historical narrative.

In addition to its historical and cultural significance, the Great Wall is an engineering marvel. The construction techniques used to build the wall varied depending on the local environment and available resources. In mountainous regions, the wall was constructed using stones and rocks, while in desert areas, rammed earth and adobe bricks were more commonly used. The builders ingeniously adapted to the challenging terrain, creating a structure that harmonized with the natural landscape while maximizing its defensive capabilities.

The Great Wall's construction also involved sophisticated logistical planning and organization. The transportation of materials, the coordination of labor, and the management of resources required an immense administrative effort. The labor force consisted of soldiers, peasants, prisoners, and conscripts, who endured harsh conditions and grueling work. The construction of the wall exacted a heavy toll on the laborers, with many losing their lives due to the strenuous labor, harsh weather, and disease. The wall's construction and maintenance were a testament to the state's ability to mobilize and manage vast human and material resources.

The Great Wall's impact on Chinese society and culture is profound. It has inspired countless works of literature, art, and folklore, becoming a symbol of perseverance, strength, and the enduring spirit of the Chinese people. The wall's presence in the collective consciousness of China is evident in its depiction in poetry, paintings, and popular culture. It serves as a reminder of the nation's historical struggles and triumphs, as well as its capacity for monumental achievement.

In modern times, the Great Wall has become a symbol of China's rich cultural heritage and a major tourist attraction. Millions of visitors from around the world come to see the wall, marvel at its scale and beauty, and learn about its history. The influx of tourists has brought economic benefits to the surrounding regions, but it has also posed challenges for the preservation and conservation of the wall. Efforts to protect and restore the Great Wall are ongoing, involving collaboration between the Chinese government, international organizations, and local communities.

The preservation of the Great Wall is a complex and multifaceted endeavor. Environmental factors such as erosion, weathering, and vegetation growth pose significant threats to the wall's integrity. Human activities, including tourism, construction, and agriculture, also impact the wall's condition. Conservation efforts aim to address these challenges through measures such as erosion control, structural reinforcement, and the regulation of tourism. Advanced technologies, such as 3D scanning and geographic information systems (GIS), are used to monitor and document the wall's condition, aiding in the development of effective preservation strategies.

The Great Wall's legacy extends beyond its physical structure. It represents a significant chapter in the history of human civilization, highlighting the ingenuity, resilience, and determination of the people who built and maintained it. The wall's construction and its role in shaping Chinese history offer valuable lessons about the complexities of empire-building, the importance of cultural exchange, and the enduring impact of monumental architecture.

Chapter 9: Teotihuacan

Teotihuacan, located in the highlands of central Mexico, is one of the most significant and enigmatic archaeological sites of the ancient world. Known as the "City of the Gods," Teotihuacan was a major urban center that flourished between the 1st and 7th centuries CE, reaching its zenith in the 4th and 5th centuries. Covering an area of about 20 square kilometers (8 square miles), it was one of the largest cities in the pre-Columbian Americas, with a population that may have exceeded 125,000 inhabitants at its peak. Despite its size and influence, much about Teotihuacan remains shrouded in mystery, including the identity of its founders, the nature of its political and social organization, and the reasons for its decline.

The city's most prominent features are its monumental pyramids, vast plazas, and complex residential compounds. The Pyramid of the Sun, the largest structure in Teotihuacan, dominates the central axis of the city, known as the Avenue of the Dead. Rising to a height of 65 meters (213 feet) and with a base measuring 225 by 225 meters (738 by 738 feet), the Pyramid of the Sun is one of the largest pyramids in the world. Built in several phases, the pyramid was constructed primarily of adobe bricks and then faced with volcanic stone. Its alignment with astronomical events, such as the summer solstice, suggests that it played a significant role in the city's religious and ceremonial life.

The Pyramid of the Moon, located at the northern end of the Avenue of the Dead, is the second-largest pyramid in Teotihuacan. This structure, standing at a height of 43 meters (141 feet), is believed to have been constructed over several centuries, with the earliest phases dating back to around 200 CE. The Pyramid of the Moon is aligned with the Cerro Gordo mountain, a feature that likely held religious significance for the inhabitants of Teotihuacan. The pyramid and its surrounding plaza were used for ceremonial purposes, including sacrificial rituals and public gatherings.

The Temple of the Feathered Serpent, also known as the Pyramid of Quetzalcoatl, is another major architectural highlight of Teotihuacan. Located in the southern part of the city, this structure is famous for its intricate and well-preserved stone carvings depicting feathered serpents and other deities. Built around 200 CE, the temple is believed to have been a center for religious ceremonies and possibly served as a political hub. The discovery of mass graves containing the remains of sacrificed individuals around the temple suggests that human sacrifice was an integral part of the city's religious practices.

Teotihuacan's urban layout was meticulously planned, with a grid system that facilitated the organization of residential, administrative, and ceremonial areas. The city's infrastructure included extensive irrigation systems, canals, and reservoirs, which supported agricultural activities and ensured a stable food supply. The residential compounds, known as apartment complexes, were multifamily dwellings that housed the city's diverse population. These complexes were often elaborately decorated with murals depicting religious themes, everyday life, and mythical creatures. The presence of workshops and markets within these compounds indicates a thriving economy based on craft production, trade, and commerce.

The social and political structure of Teotihuacan remains a subject of debate among scholars. Unlike other contemporary Mesoamerican cities, such as Tikal and Copan, Teotihuacan lacks clear evidence of centralized royal authority, such as royal tombs or palatial structures. Some researchers propose that the city was governed by a collective or oligarchic system, with power distributed among various elite groups or lineages. Others suggest that a powerful priesthood or military elite may have held sway over the city's affairs. The absence of written records further complicates the understanding of Teotihuacan's political organization and the identity of its rulers.

Teotihuacan's influence extended far beyond its immediate vicinity. The city's strategic location along major trade routes facilitated the exchange of goods, ideas, and cultural practices with distant regions. Teotihuacan-style pottery, obsidian artifacts, and architectural motifs have been found at various sites throughout Mesoamerica, including the Maya lowlands, the Gulf Coast, and the Oaxaca Valley. This widespread distribution of Teotihuacan artifacts suggests that the city played a central role in regional trade networks and cultural interactions.

The city's religious and cultural impact is also evident in the spread of Teotihuacan iconography and architectural styles. The Feathered Serpent deity, prominently featured in Teotihuacan art and architecture, became a central figure in the religious pantheons of later Mesoamerican civilizations, including the Maya and the Aztec. The use of talud-tablero architecture, characterized by a sloping base (talud) supporting a vertical panel (tablero), became a hallmark of Teotihuacan influence and was adopted by various cultures across Mesoamerica.

Despite its impressive achievements, Teotihuacan began to decline in the late 6th century CE. The reasons for this decline are not fully understood but likely involve a combination of internal and external factors. Environmental changes, such as prolonged droughts, may have strained the city's agricultural resources and water supply. Social unrest, political instability, and external invasions could have further weakened the city's cohesion and security. By the 7th century, Teotihuacan had largely been abandoned, and its once-thriving urban center fell into ruins.

The legacy of Teotihuacan endured long after its decline. The city's monumental architecture and religious significance continued to inspire later Mesoamerican civilizations. The Aztecs, who rose to power in the 14th century, held Teotihuacan in great reverence, believing it to be the birthplace of the gods. The name "Teotihuacan," meaning "the place where gods were born," reflects this deep cultural and spiritual connection. The Aztecs conducted pilgrimages to the ancient city and incorporated its myths and deities into their own religious practices.

Modern archaeological research has greatly expanded our understanding of Teotihuacan. Excavations, surveys, and advanced technologies such as ground-penetrating radar and remote sensing have revealed new insights into the city's layout, construction techniques, and social organization. For example, the discovery of a tunnel beneath the Pyramid of the Feathered Serpent, filled with artifacts and offerings, has provided valuable information about the city's religious practices and the symbolic importance of its architecture.

Teotihuacan's art and architecture continue to captivate scholars and the public alike. The murals, sculptures, and pottery produced by Teotihuacan artisans are renowned for their craftsmanship and aesthetic appeal. These artworks often depict complex religious scenes, cosmological symbols, and mythical beings, offering glimpses into the spiritual and cultural life of the city's inhabitants. The use of vibrant colors, geometric patterns, and naturalistic forms reflects the artistic sophistication and creative vision of Teotihuacan society.

The preservation and conservation of Teotihuacan are ongoing challenges. The site faces threats from environmental degradation, urban encroachment, and tourism. Efforts to protect and restore the ancient city involve collaboration between the Mexican government, international organizations, and local communities. Conservation initiatives focus on stabilizing and repairing the fragile structures, mitigating the impact of tourism, and promoting sustainable practices that balance preservation with public access and education.

Teotihuacan's inclusion as a UNESCO World Heritage site in 1987 underscores its global significance as a cultural and historical landmark. The recognition of Teotihuacan as a heritage site highlights the importance of preserving its unique legacy for future generations. The ancient city continues to attract visitors from around the world, who come to explore its awe-inspiring pyramids, plazas, and murals, and to connect with the rich history and heritage of Mesoamerica.

Chapter 10: Acropolis of Athens

The Acropolis of Athens is an ancient citadel located on a rocky outcrop above the city of Athens, Greece. It is perhaps the most significant and recognizable symbol of classical Greek culture, representing the zenith of Athenian power, art, and architecture during the 5th century BCE. The Acropolis is home to several ancient structures of great architectural and historic significance, the most famous of which is the Parthenon. These buildings are regarded as some of the greatest achievements in Western civilization, reflecting the values, aesthetics, and technological advancements of the time.

The history of the Acropolis dates back to the Neolithic period, but it became most prominent during the 5th century BCE, when Athens was at the height of its power. The strategic location of the Acropolis, on a high, rocky hill, made it a natural fortress and a center of the city's religious life. The earliest structures on the Acropolis were likely built in the Mycenaean period (circa 1600-1100 BCE), but the most significant constructions were initiated in the mid-5th century BCE under the leadership of Pericles, during what is often referred to as the Golden Age of Athens.

Pericles, an influential statesman, orator, and general of Athens, oversaw an ambitious building program aimed at glorifying the city and demonstrating its cultural and political supremacy. This building program resulted in the construction of the Parthenon, the Erechtheion, the Temple of Athena Nike, and the Propylaea, each of which was designed by some of the most renowned architects and sculptors of the time. These structures not only served religious and ceremonial purposes but also symbolized the wealth, power, and artistic excellence of Athens.

The Parthenon, dedicated to Athena Parthenos (the Virgin Athena), the patron goddess of Athens, is the most iconic and grandest structure on the Acropolis. Designed by the architects Ictinus and

Callicrates and adorned with sculptures by the artist Phidias, the Parthenon epitomizes the ideals of classical Greek architecture. Constructed between 447 and 432 BCE, the Parthenon is a Doric temple with some Ionic elements, reflecting a blend of architectural styles. It is renowned for its perfect proportions, achieved through subtle adjustments such as the slight curvature of the columns and the stylobate (the platform on which the columns stand), which correct optical illusions and create a harmonious appearance.

The Parthenon housed a massive statue of Athena Parthenos, made of gold and ivory, also crafted by Phidias. This statue was a symbol of the city's wealth and devotion to their goddess. The temple's decorative sculptures, including the metopes, frieze, and pediments, depicted various mythological scenes, such as the Panathenaic procession, the battle between the Lapiths and the Centaurs, and the birth of Athena. These sculptures are considered masterpieces of classical art, demonstrating a high level of skill in depicting movement, anatomy, and emotion.

Adjacent to the Parthenon is the Erechtheion, a temple dedicated to both Athena and Poseidon, constructed between 421 and 406 BCE. The Erechtheion is notable for its complex and asymmetrical design, which was necessary to accommodate the uneven terrain and the various religious shrines it encompassed. One of its most famous features is the Porch of the Caryatids, where six sculpted female figures (the Caryatids) serve as supporting columns. These elegant and lifelike statues exemplify the skill of Athenian sculptors and add to the unique character of the temple.

The Temple of Athena Nike, situated on the southwest corner of the Acropolis, was built around 427-424 BCE to celebrate the military victories of Athens and honor Athena as the goddess of victory. This small Ionic temple, designed by the architect Callicrates, is distinguished by its graceful proportions and decorative frieze depicting scenes of battle and victory. The temple's location, overlooking the city and the surrounding landscape, symbolized the protection and favor of Athena.

The Propylaea, the monumental gateway to the Acropolis, was constructed between 437 and 432 BCE under the direction of the architect Mnesicles. This grand entrance, designed in the Doric style with some Ionic elements, served both a functional and symbolic purpose, providing an impressive approach to the sacred precinct. The central hall of the Propylaea was flanked by two wings, one of which housed the Pinakotheke, a gallery for displaying paintings. The scale and complexity of the Propylaea reflected the importance of the Acropolis as a religious and cultural center.

In addition to these major buildings, the Acropolis also contained numerous smaller structures, altars, and statues dedicated to various deities and heroes. The entire site was a focal point of Athenian religious life, hosting important festivals, rituals, and ceremonies, such as the Panathenaic Festival, which honored Athena with processions, sacrifices, and athletic competitions.

The Acropolis and its buildings underwent various modifications and restorations over the centuries. During the Hellenistic and Roman periods, additional structures and monuments were added, and the existing buildings were maintained and repaired. However, the site also suffered significant damage and alterations, particularly during the early Christian and Byzantine periods, when many of the pagan temples were converted into churches. The Parthenon, for instance, was transformed into a Christian church dedicated to the Virgin Mary in the 6th century CE.

The Acropolis endured further destruction during the Ottoman period, particularly during the Venetian siege of Athens in 1687. An explosion caused by a Venetian bombardment severely damaged the Parthenon, which was being used as a gunpowder magazine by the Ottomans. Despite these devastations, the Acropolis continued to be a symbol of cultural and historical significance.

In the 19th century, following Greece's independence from the Ottoman Empire, efforts to restore and preserve the Acropolis began in earnest. Archaeologists and architects undertook extensive excavations and conservation projects to stabilize and protect the ancient structures. These efforts have continued into the present day, with ongoing restoration work aimed at preserving the Acropolis for future generations while ensuring that it remains accessible to scholars, tourists, and the general public.

The Acropolis of Athens holds a central place in the study of ancient Greek art and architecture. It provides invaluable insights into the political, religious, and cultural life of classical Athens. The architectural innovations and artistic achievements exemplified by the buildings and sculptures of the Acropolis have had a profound influence on subsequent architectural styles and artistic traditions, both in the Western world and beyond.

Moreover, the Acropolis has come to symbolize the enduring legacy of classical Greek civilization. It represents the ideals of democracy, humanism, and artistic excellence that were championed by the Athenians. The philosophical, political, and artistic contributions of classical Athens continue to resonate in contemporary society, and the Acropolis serves as a tangible reminder of this rich heritage.

The site of the Acropolis has also been a source of inspiration for various cultural and intellectual movements throughout history. During the Renaissance, for example, the rediscovery of classical Greek and Roman art and architecture spurred a renewed interest in the ideals of antiquity, leading to the revival of classical forms in art, architecture, and literature. The Neoclassical movement of the 18th and 19th centuries similarly drew inspiration from the Acropolis, influencing the design of buildings, monuments, and public spaces around the world.

Today, the Acropolis of Athens is a UNESCO World Heritage site and one of the most visited tourist destinations in the world. Its iconic structures, particularly the Parthenon, attract millions of visitors each year, who come to marvel at the architectural and artistic achievements of ancient Greece. The Acropolis Museum, opened in 2009, houses many of the artifacts and sculptures found on the site, providing context and interpretation for the ancient remains.

The preservation of the Acropolis poses ongoing challenges, particularly in the face of environmental threats such as pollution, weathering, and seismic activity. The Greek government, in collaboration with international organizations and experts, continues to implement conservation strategies aimed at safeguarding the site while balancing the needs of tourism and public access. These efforts reflect a commitment to preserving the Acropolis not only as a historical and cultural monument but also as a symbol of the enduring values and achievements of human civilization.

Chapter 11: The Sphinx

The Great Sphinx of Giza, an iconic symbol of ancient Egypt, is a colossal limestone statue situated on the Giza Plateau, near the Great Pyramids. This enigmatic monument, with the body of a lion and the head of a human, is one of the oldest and most mysterious structures in the world. Carved directly from the bedrock of the plateau, the Sphinx has been a source of fascination and speculation for millennia, inspiring numerous myths, legends, and scholarly debates regarding its origins, purpose, and symbolism.

The Great Sphinx is believed to have been constructed during the Old Kingdom of Egypt, around 2500 BCE, during the reign of Pharaoh Khafre (also known as Chephren), who ruled from approximately 2558 to 2532 BCE. It is generally accepted among Egyptologists that the Sphinx was created to serve as a guardian of the Giza Plateau and as a representation of royal power and divine protection. The head of the Sphinx is often thought to be a depiction of Khafre himself, emphasizing the pharaoh's role as a god-king and the protector of his people.

The Sphinx measures about 73 meters (240 feet) in length, 20 meters (66 feet) in height, and 19 meters (62 feet) in width, making it one of the largest monolithic statues in the world. Its sheer size and the complexity of its construction have led to various theories about the techniques and labor force involved in its creation. It is believed that thousands of laborers, including skilled artisans and workers, were employed to carve the statue from a single limestone outcrop. The stone was likely quarried using copper tools, such as chisels and hammers, and the monument's features were meticulously shaped to achieve its final form.

The face of the Sphinx, although eroded over time, still retains some of its original features, including the characteristic headdress (the nemes) and traces of the royal beard. The eyes, nose, and lips were once finely detailed, conveying a sense of majesty and authority. However, the nose of the Sphinx is notably missing, having been damaged or deliberately removed in antiquity. Various stories and theories exist about the cause of this damage, but there is no definitive evidence to support any single explanation.

The body of the Sphinx, which represents a lion, symbolizes strength and power, qualities that were associated with the pharaoh and the sun god Ra. The lion's form was also believed to offer protection against malevolent forces, reinforcing the idea of the Sphinx as a guardian of the sacred site. The combination of human and lion elements in the Sphinx's design reflects the ancient Egyptian belief in the divine nature of the pharaoh, who was seen as both a human ruler and a god on earth.

Over the centuries, the Sphinx has undergone numerous restorations and conservation efforts to address the effects of natural erosion and human activity. The statue has been buried in sand for much of its history, which helped to protect it from further damage but also obscured it from view. The first recorded excavation of the Sphinx dates back to the 18th Dynasty of Egypt, during the reign of Pharaoh Thutmose IV (circa 1401-1391 BCE). According to an inscription known as the Dream Stele, which was erected between the Sphinx's paws, Thutmose IV had a dream in which the Sphinx spoke to him, promising him the throne of Egypt if he cleared away the sand that had buried its body. Thutmose IV fulfilled this task and subsequently became pharaoh, erecting the stele as a testament to his divine encounter and the Sphinx's protective power.

In more recent times, significant restoration efforts have been undertaken to preserve the Sphinx. These efforts have included repairing cracks and fissures in the limestone, reinforcing weakened areas with modern materials, and implementing measures to prevent further erosion. Despite these efforts, the Sphinx remains vulnerable to environmental factors, such as pollution, groundwater, and temperature fluctuations, which continue to pose challenges for its preservation.

The Great Sphinx has inspired a wealth of mythology and speculation, both in antiquity and in modern times. In ancient Egyptian mythology, the Sphinx was associated with several deities, including Ra-Horakhty (a form of the sun god Horus), who was depicted as a falcon-headed god with solar attributes. The Sphinx's role as a solar deity and its eastward orientation, facing the rising sun, reinforced its symbolic connection to the sun god and the concept of rebirth and renewal.

In Greek mythology, the Sphinx was a creature with the body of a lion, the head of a woman, and the wings of an eagle. It was known for posing riddles to travelers and devouring those who could not answer correctly. The most famous myth involving the Greek Sphinx is the story of Oedipus, who successfully answered the Sphinx's riddle and thus freed the city of Thebes from its curse. This mythological depiction, although different from the Egyptian Sphinx, highlights the creature's association with mystery, knowledge, and guardianship.

Modern interpretations of the Sphinx have also generated a variety of theories, ranging from the plausible to the speculative. Some researchers have proposed that the Sphinx predates the Old Kingdom and was originally constructed by a more ancient civilization, possibly as early as 10,000 BCE. This theory, often associated with the work of geologist Robert Schoch, is based on the observation of weathering patterns on the Sphinx's body, which some believe are indicative of prolonged exposure to water erosion rather than mere wind and sand.

Other fringe theories suggest that the Sphinx has hidden chambers or passages beneath it, possibly containing undiscovered treasures or ancient knowledge. While these claims have fueled popular imagination and numerous exploratory attempts, mainstream archaeology has not found substantial evidence to support such theories. Nevertheless, the allure of the Sphinx's mysteries continues to captivate researchers and enthusiasts alike.

The Great Sphinx also holds a prominent place in modern culture, symbolizing the enduring legacy of ancient Egypt and its achievements. It has been featured in countless works of art, literature, and film, often serving as a powerful icon of ancient wisdom, mystery, and resilience. The image of the Sphinx, alongside the pyramids, has become synonymous with Egypt itself, attracting millions of tourists and scholars to the Giza Plateau each year.

In addition to its cultural and historical significance, the Sphinx has been a subject of scientific inquiry, particularly in the fields of archaeology, geology, and Egyptology. Researchers have studied the Sphinx to gain insights into ancient construction techniques, the social and religious practices of the Old Kingdom, and the broader context of Egyptian civilization. Advances in technology, such as ground-penetrating radar and 3D scanning, have enabled more detailed and non-invasive examinations of the statue, contributing to our understanding of its construction and condition.

The preservation of the Sphinx is an ongoing priority for Egyptian authorities and the international community. Conservation initiatives focus on mitigating the impact of environmental factors, such as groundwater seepage, air pollution, and temperature variations, which can accelerate the deterioration of the limestone. Protective measures, including barriers, drainage systems, and controlled access, aim to safeguard the Sphinx while allowing for continued study and public appreciation.

The Great Sphinx of Giza, with its imposing presence and enigmatic expression, continues to inspire awe and curiosity. As a monument that has witnessed the rise and fall of civilizations, it stands as a testament to the ingenuity and creativity of ancient Egypt. Its enduring mystery and grandeur ensure that the Sphinx will remain a subject of fascination and reverence for generations to come.

Chapter 12: Temple of Karnak

The Temple of Karnak, situated on the east bank of the Nile River in Luxor (ancient Thebes), Egypt, is one of the most magnificent and expansive temple complexes ever constructed. It stands as a testament to the architectural, artistic, and religious achievements of ancient Egypt, serving as a central place of worship for over two millennia. The construction of the Karnak Temple complex spanned approximately 2,000 years, with contributions from numerous pharaohs, each leaving their mark on this vast religious site dedicated primarily to the Theban triad of deities: Amun, Mut, and Khonsu.

The site of Karnak covers more than 100 hectares (247 acres) and is divided into four main precincts: the Precinct of Amun-Re, the Precinct of Mut, the Precinct of Montu, and the now largely destroyed Temple of Amenhotep IV (Akhenaten). The largest and most significant of these is the Precinct of Amun-Re, which is often simply referred to as the Temple of Karnak. This precinct alone is home to some of the most famous and awe-inspiring structures within the complex, showcasing the grandeur and complexity of ancient Egyptian temple architecture.

The history of Karnak dates back to the Middle Kingdom (circa 2055-1650 BCE), with the earliest construction attributed to Pharaoh Senusret I (circa 1971-1926 BCE). However, the majority of the monumental buildings seen today were erected during the New Kingdom (circa 1550-1070 BCE), a period marked by the height of Theban power and influence. Pharaohs such as Thutmose I, Hatshepsut, Thutmose III, Amenhotep III, and Ramses II were instrumental in expanding and embellishing the temple complex, each contributing to its architectural and artistic splendor.

At the heart of the Karnak complex is the Great Hypostyle Hall, a breathtaking architectural feat covering an area of approximately 5,000 square meters (54,000 square feet). This hall, constructed during the reigns of Seti I and his son Ramses II (circa 1290-1224 BCE), contains 134 massive columns arranged in 16 rows. The central columns, standing at 24 meters (79 feet) tall, are capped with open papyrus flower capitals, while the shorter columns in the side aisles have closed bud capitals. The sheer scale and grandeur of the Hypostyle Hall, with its forest of columns and intricate carvings, leave visitors in awe of the ancient builders' ingenuity and craftsmanship.

The walls and columns of the Hypostyle Hall are adorned with detailed reliefs and inscriptions depicting scenes of religious rituals, military victories, and offerings to the gods. These carvings provide invaluable insights into the religious beliefs, political events, and daily life of ancient Egypt. The reliefs also highlight the pharaohs' divine right to rule and their close relationship with the gods, emphasizing the temple's role as a center of religious and political power.

Another notable feature of the Karnak complex is the Sacred Lake, a large, rectangular basin of water measuring approximately 120 by 77 meters (394 by 253 feet). The lake, created during the reign of Thutmose III (circa 1479-1425 BCE), was used for ritual purposes, including purification rites performed by the priests. The water symbolized the primeval waters of creation, and the lake's presence within the temple complex underscored the importance of water in ancient Egyptian religious practices.

The Temple of Karnak also houses a series of massive pylons (gateway towers) that mark the entrances to different sections of the temple. These pylons, often decorated with scenes of the pharaoh's triumphs and offerings to the gods, served both a symbolic and defensive purpose. The largest of these pylons is the First Pylon, which stands at the entrance to the Precinct of Amun-Re. Though incomplete, this pylon was originally intended to be part of a grand forecourt and ceremonial approach to the temple.

The central sanctuary of the Precinct of Amun-Re, known as the Holy of Holies, was the most sacred part of the temple, housing the statue of the god Amun. Access to this inner sanctum was restricted to the high priests and the pharaoh, who performed daily rituals to honor and appease the deity. The sanctuary was surrounded by smaller chapels and shrines dedicated to other gods and goddesses, creating a complex network of interconnected spaces for worship and ritual.

Throughout its long history, the Temple of Karnak was not only a religious center but also a hub of political and economic activity. The temple complex was supported by vast agricultural estates, workshops, and storerooms, which provided the resources needed to sustain the large priesthood and support the temple's extensive building and maintenance projects. The wealth and influence of the Karnak priesthood grew significantly during the New Kingdom, at times rivaling the power of the pharaohs themselves.

One of the most remarkable aspects of the Karnak complex is the way in which it evolved over time, with each pharaoh adding their own contributions to the site. Queen Hatshepsut, one of the most famous female pharaohs, commissioned numerous building projects at Karnak, including the construction of the Red Chapel (Chapelle Rouge), a barque shrine for the sacred boat of Amun. Hatshepsut's reign (circa 1479-1458 BCE) was marked by significant architectural achievements, and her contributions to Karnak are among the most notable.

Thutmose III, often regarded as one of ancient Egypt's greatest military leaders, also left a lasting legacy at Karnak. He constructed the Festival Hall (Akh-Menu), a unique building with a series of chambers and colonnades, which served as a venue for the celebration of the king's Sed festival, a jubilee event marking the renewal of the pharaoh's reign. Thutmose III's additions to Karnak reflect his desire to commemorate his military successes and reinforce his divine right to rule.

The later pharaohs of the New Kingdom, including Amenhotep III and Ramses II, continued to enhance the grandeur of Karnak.

Amenhotep III's reign (circa 1390-1352 BCE) was characterized by a flourishing of art and architecture, and his contributions to Karnak include the construction of the magnificent Third Pylon and a series of monumental statues. Ramses II, known for his extensive building projects and military campaigns, added to the Hypostyle Hall and erected colossal statues and obelisks throughout the temple complex.

The decline of the New Kingdom marked a period of reduced activity at Karnak, but the temple complex continued to be an important religious site during the later periods of Egyptian history. The Ptolemaic and Roman rulers of Egypt also made contributions to Karnak, reflecting the continued significance of the site in the religious and cultural landscape of Egypt.

The Temple of Karnak has been the subject of extensive archaeological study and restoration efforts. The French Institute of Oriental Archaeology (IFAO) and the Egyptian Ministry of Antiquities have played significant roles in the excavation, documentation, and preservation of the site. These efforts have uncovered a wealth of artifacts, inscriptions, and architectural details that have deepened our understanding of the temple's history and significance.

Today, the Temple of Karnak is a UNESCO World Heritage site and one of the most popular tourist destinations in Egypt. Visitors from around the world come to marvel at the sheer scale and grandeur of the temple complex, exploring its vast halls, courtyards, and sanctuaries. The site offers a unique glimpse into the religious, political, and artistic achievements of ancient Egypt, providing a tangible connection to a civilization that has fascinated humanity for centuries.

The ongoing preservation and study of Karnak are crucial to ensuring that future generations can continue to experience and learn from this remarkable testament to human ingenuity and devotion. The Temple of Karnak stands as a powerful reminder of the enduring legacy of ancient Egypt and its contributions to the cultural and historical heritage of the world.

Chapter 13: Alhambra

The Alhambra, a magnificent palace and fortress complex in Granada, Spain, is one of the most emblematic examples of Moorish architecture. It was originally constructed as a small fortress in 889 AD on the remains of Roman fortifications, but it was largely ignored until its ruins were renovated and rebuilt in the mid-13th century by the Nasrid emir Mohammed ben Al-Ahmar of the Emirate of Granada, who transformed it into a royal palace. The Alhambra stands as a testament to the intricate artistry and sophisticated engineering of the Islamic Golden Age, blending Islamic art, culture, and science.

The complex's name, Alhambra, derives from the Arabic "Al-Qal'a al-Hamra," meaning "The Red Castle," a reference to the reddish hue of its walls, constructed from the locally sourced iron-infused clay. The Alhambra's strategic location atop the al-Sabika hill provides commanding views of the city of Granada and the surrounding fertile plain of the Vega, making it both a formidable fortress and a symbol of Nasrid power and opulence.

The Alhambra encompasses an area of about 142,000 square meters and comprises several distinct parts, including the Alcazaba (the fortress), the Nasrid Palaces, and the Generalife. The Alcazaba is the oldest part of the Alhambra and served as the military stronghold. Its robust fortifications, including massive walls and imposing towers such as the Torre de la Vela and the Torre del Homenaje, were designed to protect the residents from invaders and offer a strategic vantage point for defense.

The Nasrid Palaces are the epitome of Islamic architectural and artistic achievement. The Mexuar, the oldest palace section, functioned as the administrative and public part of the complex, where the sultans held court. The Mexuar Hall, with its intricate stucco work, tile mosaics, and wooden ceilings, is a prime example of the sophisticated decorative arts of the time. Adjoining the Mexuar is the Comares

Palace, named after its main tower, the Torre de Comares. This palace includes the Hall of the Ambassadors, the largest room in the Alhambra, used for important ceremonies and diplomatic receptions. Its walls are adorned with elaborate calligraphy and geometric patterns, embodying the Islamic artistic principle of aniconism, or the avoidance of figural representations.

The Palace of the Lions, another significant part of the Nasrid Palaces, is renowned for its central courtyard, the Court of the Lions, which features a famous marble fountain supported by twelve stylized lion statues. This palace was the private living quarters of the Nasrid emirs and their families. The Hall of the Abencerrajes and the Hall of the Kings are particularly notable for their muqarnas (honeycomb) vaulting, a hallmark of Islamic architecture, creating a stunning interplay of light and shadow that enhances the sense of divine beauty and transcendence.

The Generalife, the summer palace and country estate of the Nasrid rulers, is another integral part of the Alhambra. Situated to the east of the main complex, it served as a retreat from the formalities of court life. The Generalife is celebrated for its lush gardens, which include the Patio de la Acequia (Court of the Water Channel), a long pool framed by flowerbeds, fountains, colonnades, and pavilions. The tranquil and meticulously designed gardens reflect the Islamic paradise garden concept, symbolizing an earthly representation of the divine garden described in the Quran.

The Alhambra's intricate tile work, stucco reliefs, and wooden inlays are testaments to the high level of craftsmanship achieved by the artisans of the Nasrid dynasty. The use of arabesques, an ornamental design consisting of intertwined flowing lines, is prevalent throughout the complex. These designs, combined with the extensive use of Arabic calligraphy featuring verses from the Quran, serve both decorative and didactic purposes, continuously reminding visitors of the spiritual and moral values of Islam.

The Alhambra's architectural style is often described as a culmination of Islamic art in Spain, characterized by its use of intricate geometric patterns, elaborate tile mosaics, and complex stucco carvings. This style influenced subsequent architectural developments in Spain and beyond, contributing to the Mudéjar style, which blends Islamic and Christian design elements.

The fall of Granada in 1492 to the Catholic Monarchs, Ferdinand and Isabella, marked the end of Muslim rule in Spain. The Alhambra was spared destruction and instead was adapted for use by the Christian rulers. Significant alterations were made, including the construction of the Renaissance-style Palace of Charles V, which stands in stark contrast to the rest of the complex. This palace, built in the 16th century, is a symbol of the Christian conquest and integration of Spanish and Moorish cultures. Its circular courtyard is an architectural anomaly within the otherwise predominantly Islamic design of the Alhambra.

Throughout the centuries, the Alhambra experienced periods of neglect and restoration. During the French occupation of Spain in the early 19th century, parts of the Alhambra were damaged, and the complex fell into disrepair. It wasn't until the mid-19th century, during the Romantic era, that the Alhambra gained renewed interest from scholars, artists, and writers, who were captivated by its beauty and historical significance. The American writer Washington Irving, who lived in the Alhambra for a time, wrote "Tales of the Alhambra," which helped popularize the site and draw attention to its preservation.

Today, the Alhambra is a UNESCO World Heritage Site and one of Spain's most visited tourist attractions. It continues to be a source of inspiration for artists, architects, and historians. The complex serves as a vivid reminder of the cultural and architectural achievements of the Islamic period in Spain and stands as a monument to the rich, diverse history of the Iberian Peninsula. The Alhambra's enduring legacy is not only its architectural splendor but also its role as a bridge between different cultures and epochs, encapsulating the confluence of Islamic and Christian civilizations in medieval Spain.

The conservation and management of the Alhambra are ongoing challenges, given the immense number of visitors and the need to preserve its delicate structures and intricate artworks. Efforts are continuously made to balance public access with the preservation of the site, ensuring that future generations can appreciate and learn from this historical and architectural marvel. The Alhambra remains a symbol of the artistic and cultural flowering of the Nasrid dynasty and a testament to the enduring legacy of the Moorish presence in Spain. Its beauty, complexity, and historical significance make it a unique and invaluable part of the world's cultural heritage.

Chapter 14: Chichen Itza

Chichen Itza, one of the most renowned archaeological sites in Mexico, is located in the eastern part of the Yucatán Peninsula. This ancient Mayan city, now a UNESCO World Heritage Site, stands as a testament to the ingenuity, architectural prowess, and astronomical knowledge of the Maya civilization. Chichen Itza was a major focal point in the Northern Maya Lowlands from the Late Classic (600–900 AD) to the Terminal Classic (800–900 AD) and into the early portion of the Postclassic period (900–1200 AD). The city's history and influence extended well into the Late Postclassic period (1200–1500 AD), and even after its decline, it remained a pilgrimage site until the arrival of the Spanish.

The name "Chichen Itza" means "At the mouth of the well of the Itza," derived from the Maya words "chi" (mouth), "chen" (well), and "Itza," the name of the Maya ethnic group that settled around this site. The presence of two large natural sinkholes, or cenotes, on the site, provided a vital water source and were considered sacred by the Maya, playing a crucial role in the city's establishment and development.

Chichen Itza's most iconic structure is the Temple of Kukulkan, also known as El Castillo. This step pyramid stands about 30 meters high and has a series of nine square terraces, culminating in a temple at the summit. Each of the pyramid's four sides has 91 steps, which, when combined with the temple platform at the top, total 365 steps, representing the days of the solar year. The pyramid is a striking example of Mayan astronomical and architectural precision. During the spring and autumn equinoxes, the setting sun casts a series of triangular shadows on the pyramid's balustrade, creating the illusion of a serpent descending the steps. This phenomenon symbolizes the return of Kukulkan, the feathered serpent deity, a central figure in Maya religion and mythology.

The Great Ball Court is another prominent feature of Chichen Itza. Measuring 168 meters in length and 70 meters in width, it is the largest and best-preserved ball court in ancient Mesoamerica. The game played here, known as the Mesoamerican ballgame, had deep ritual significance. The court's walls are adorned with intricate carvings depicting scenes of the game, including players in elaborate attire and the ritual decapitation of the losing team, a practice believed to appease the gods and ensure agricultural fertility.

Adjacent to the Great Ball Court is the Temple of the Jaguars, which features a platform adorned with a carved jaguar throne and murals depicting military and ceremonial scenes. Nearby, the Tzompantli, or Skull Platform, is a stone structure covered with bas-reliefs of skulls, a chilling reminder of the site's ritual sacrifices and the Maya's complex relationship with death and the afterlife.

The Sacred Cenote, also known as the Well of Sacrifice, is another critical element of Chichen Itza. This large, natural sinkhole was used for ceremonial purposes, including human sacrifices. Archaeological excavations have recovered a wealth of artifacts from the cenote, including gold, jade, pottery, and human remains, offering insights into the religious practices and material culture of the Maya.

Chichen Itza is also home to the Temple of the Warriors, a large stepped pyramid flanked by rows of carved columns depicting warriors. The temple complex includes the Group of the Thousand Columns, an extensive colonnade that once supported a large roof structure, possibly a marketplace or assembly hall. The temple's summit houses a Chac Mool statue, a reclining figure with a bowl on its stomach, believed to have been used in sacrificial rituals.

The Osario, or High Priest's Grave, is a smaller pyramid similar in design to El Castillo but built over a natural cave. This structure was used as a tomb for high-ranking individuals, and its interior chambers contain several burial sites. The structure's alignment and construction further demonstrate the Maya's advanced understanding of astronomy and the natural landscape.

The Caracol, or Observatory, is a circular tower on a rectangular platform, believed to have been used by the Maya priests for astronomical observations. The structure's design, with its windows aligned with various celestial events, underscores the Maya's sophisticated knowledge of astronomy and its integration into their architectural planning and religious practices.

Chichen Itza's economic and political power peaked during the Terminal Classic period, making it a significant center for trade, politics, and military might. The city's strategic location allowed it to control trade routes extending across the Yucatán Peninsula, facilitating the exchange of goods such as obsidian, jade, textiles, and pottery. This economic prosperity supported the construction of monumental architecture and the development of an intricate social and political structure.

Despite its prominence, Chichen Itza experienced periods of decline and resurgence. Around 1000 AD, internal strife and climatic changes likely contributed to its decline, although it remained a vital cultural and religious center. The reasons for its eventual abandonment in the late 13th century remain a topic of scholarly debate, with theories ranging from ecological stress and drought to political upheaval and conquest by rival groups.

The arrival of the Spanish in the 16th century marked a new chapter in the history of Chichen Itza. Spanish chroniclers recorded the site, but it remained largely abandoned until the 19th century when explorers and archaeologists began to study its ruins. John Lloyd Stephens and Frederick Catherwood's documentation in the 1840s brought international attention to Chichen Itza, sparking renewed interest and extensive archaeological research.

Today, Chichen Itza is a symbol of the Maya civilization's enduring legacy and a major tourist attraction, drawing millions of visitors each year. The site's preservation and conservation are ongoing challenges, given the impacts of tourism and natural weathering. Efforts by the Mexican government and international organizations aim to protect and restore Chichen Itza's monuments, ensuring that future generations can continue to marvel at its splendor.

The cultural and historical significance of Chichen Itza extends beyond its impressive architecture. It embodies the achievements of the Maya in various fields, including mathematics, astronomy, art, and engineering. The city's layout and structures reflect the Maya's complex social organization, religious beliefs, and interactions with the environment. The study of Chichen Itza provides valuable insights into the Maya civilization's contributions to human knowledge and cultural heritage.

Chapter 15: Temple of Luxor

The Temple of Luxor, situated on the east bank of the Nile River in the city of Luxor (ancient Thebes), Egypt, is one of the most remarkable and historically significant temple complexes of ancient Egypt. It stands as a testament to the grandeur of the New Kingdom era, particularly reflecting the reigns of the Pharaohs Amenhotep III and Ramses II. The construction of the temple began around 1400 BCE under the orders of Amenhotep III and was later expanded by Ramses II in the 13th century BCE. The Temple of Luxor was dedicated primarily to the rejuvenation of kingship and the worship of the Theban Triad of gods: Amun, Mut, and their son Khonsu.

The temple's architecture is a stunning example of the classical Egyptian style, featuring massive pylons, courtyards, hypostyle halls, and sanctuaries adorned with intricate carvings and hieroglyphics. The entrance to the temple is marked by a majestic pylon constructed by Ramses II, standing 24 meters high and originally flanked by six colossal statues of the pharaoh, two seated and four standing, though only two of these statues remain intact today. In front of the pylon once stood a pair of obelisks, though only one remains at the site; the other was gifted to France in 1833 and now stands in the Place de la Concorde in Paris.

Beyond the pylon lies the first courtyard, known as the Court of Ramses II. This spacious courtyard, measuring approximately 57 by 51 meters, is surrounded by a double row of papyrus columns, each column standing about 16 meters high. The walls of the courtyard are adorned with vivid reliefs depicting Ramses II's military campaigns, including the famous Battle of Kadesh, as well as scenes of religious rituals and offerings to the gods.

Following the Court of Ramses II is the Colonnade of Amenhotep III, a grand processional avenue that leads to the inner parts of the temple. This colonnade is a masterpiece of ancient Egyptian architecture, consisting of 14 massive papyrus columns arranged in two rows, each column rising to a height of 19 meters. The colonnade was designed to represent the primeval mound of creation, a recurring theme in Egyptian temple architecture symbolizing the emergence of order from chaos.

The colonnade leads to the Court of Amenhotep III, a rectangular courtyard measuring about 45 by 56 meters. This courtyard is similarly surrounded by papyrus-bud columns and is open to the sky, allowing sunlight to illuminate the central altar where offerings were made. The walls of the court are intricately decorated with scenes depicting Amenhotep III's divine birth and coronation, emphasizing the pharaoh's divine right to rule and his close relationship with the gods.

Beyond the Court of Amenhotep III lies the hypostyle hall, a grand hall filled with 32 columns arranged in four rows. This hall served as a transitional space leading to the more sacred areas of the temple. The columns are adorned with carvings of lotus and papyrus plants, symbolizing Upper and Lower Egypt, and the ceiling is decorated with astronomical scenes representing the sky goddess Nut.

The innermost part of the temple is the sanctuary, which housed the sacred barque (boat) of Amun. This area was considered the most sacred part of the temple, accessible only to the high priests and the pharaoh. The sanctuary consists of several smaller chambers, including the barque shrine, which was rebuilt by Alexander the Great in the 4th century BCE. The walls of the sanctuary are covered with scenes depicting the divine birth of the pharaoh, his interactions with the gods, and various religious rituals.

The Temple of Luxor was not only a place of worship but also played a crucial role in the annual Opet Festival, a major religious festival in ancient Thebes. During this festival, the statues of the Theban Triad were carried in a grand procession from the Temple of Karnak to the Temple of Luxor, symbolizing the divine rejuvenation of the pharaoh and the fertility of the land. The procession, accompanied by priests, musicians, dancers, and a large crowd of worshippers, would travel along the Avenue of Sphinxes, a 2.7-kilometer-long road lined with hundreds of sphinx statues connecting the two temples. The Opet Festival was a time of great celebration, with feasting, music, and dancing, reinforcing the bond between the people, their gods, and their king.

The Avenue of Sphinxes, which originally linked the Temple of Luxor with the Temple of Karnak, is an impressive feat of ancient engineering and artistry. The avenue was lined with over 1,300 sphinx statues, each carved from a single block of sandstone and depicting a lion's body with a human head, symbolizing the pharaoh's power and divine protection. Recent restoration efforts have uncovered significant portions of the avenue, allowing visitors to walk the ancient path once again and gain a deeper understanding of the grandeur and significance of this sacred route.

Throughout its long history, the Temple of Luxor underwent several modifications and expansions by successive pharaohs, including Tutankhamun, Horemheb, and even Alexander the Great, who sought to associate themselves with the glory of the New Kingdom rulers and the divine legacy of Amun. The temple's importance continued into the Roman period when it was incorporated into the Roman city of Thebes. During this time, a Roman military camp was established within the temple precinct, and several modifications were made to accommodate Roman religious practices. The remains of a Roman chapel dedicated to the cult of the imperial family can still be seen within the temple complex.

In the early Christian period, parts of the temple were converted into a church, and many of the ancient reliefs were defaced or covered with plaster as Christian iconography replaced the pagan imagery. Despite these changes, the Temple of Luxor remained a vital center of religious and cultural activity throughout its history.

In the Islamic period, a mosque dedicated to the Sufi saint Abu Haggag was built within the temple complex, and it continues to be an active place of worship today. The mosque, which dates back to the 13th century, is an integral part of the temple's history and adds to the site's rich tapestry of cultural and religious continuity.

The Temple of Luxor's preservation and restoration have been ongoing efforts, with significant archaeological work conducted since the 19th century. Early explorers such as Giovanni Battista Belzoni, John Gardner Wilkinson, and later French and Egyptian archaeologists made important discoveries that contributed to our understanding of the site. Today, the temple is a major tourist attraction, drawing visitors from around the world who come to marvel at its grandeur and learn about the ancient civilization that built it.

The Temple of Luxor is not just an architectural masterpiece; it is a living testament to the religious, political, and cultural life of ancient Egypt. Its walls and columns tell stories of divine kingship, cosmic order, and the relationship between the gods and humanity. The temple's alignment with the sun and stars reflects the ancient Egyptians' deep understanding of astronomy and their belief in the interconnectedness of the earthly and divine realms.

Chapter 16: Hagia Sophia

Hagia Sophia, known in Greek as "Holy Wisdom," is an architectural masterpiece located in Istanbul, Turkey. It has a rich and multifaceted history that spans over 1,500 years and reflects the religious, political, and cultural transformations of the region. Initially constructed as a Christian cathedral in the 6th century, it later became a mosque, and today it stands as a museum and a symbol of Byzantine and Ottoman grandeur. Its architectural innovation, stunning mosaics, and historical significance make Hagia Sophia a unique and invaluable monument of world heritage.

The construction of Hagia Sophia was ordered by the Byzantine Emperor Justinian I, and it was designed by the architects Anthemius of Tralles and Isidore of Miletus. Construction began in 532 AD and was completed in 537 AD, an astonishingly short period of five years. The edifice was intended to surpass the grandeur of all previous churches and to symbolize the might and piety of the Byzantine Empire. Upon its completion, Hagia Sophia was the largest cathedral in the world and remained so for nearly a thousand years.

The design of Hagia Sophia is a marvel of engineering and architectural ingenuity. The central feature of the structure is its massive dome, which spans 31 meters in diameter and rises 55 meters above the floor. This dome was an engineering breakthrough and is considered one of the greatest achievements of Byzantine architecture. It is supported by pendentives, triangular sections of vaulting that allow the circular base of the dome to rest on a square supporting structure. This innovative use of pendentives distributes the weight of the dome evenly and allows for an open and airy interior space, giving the illusion that the dome is suspended from heaven.

The interior of Hagia Sophia is richly decorated with mosaics, marble pillars, and gold accents, creating an atmosphere of divine opulence. The mosaics, many of which date from the 9th to the 12th centuries, are among the finest examples of Byzantine art. They depict religious figures such as Christ Pantocrator, the Virgin Mary, and various saints, as well as emperors and empresses. These mosaics are characterized by their intricate detail, vibrant colors, and the use of gold tesserae, which reflect light and create a shimmering effect that enhances the sacred ambiance of the space.

One of the most significant mosaics in Hagia Sophia is the Deesis mosaic, located on the upper gallery. This mosaic, dating from the 13th century, depicts Christ flanked by the Virgin Mary and John the Baptist in a powerful and expressive style that represents a high point of Byzantine artistry. Another notable mosaic is the apse mosaic, which shows the Virgin Mary holding the Christ Child, a common theme in Byzantine iconography that emphasizes the humanity and divinity of Jesus.

Hagia Sophia's history as a Christian cathedral lasted until 1453, when Constantinople was conquered by the Ottoman Turks under Sultan Mehmed II. Following the conquest, Hagia Sophia was converted into a mosque, a transformation that involved several architectural and decorative changes. Minarets were added to the exterior to call the faithful to prayer, and Christian iconography was either removed or plastered over, though fortunately, many mosaics were preserved under this plaster.

The Ottomans also made structural modifications to reinforce the building, including the addition of buttresses to support the weight of the dome. The mihrab, the niche indicating the direction of Mecca, was installed in the apse, and the minbar, the pulpit from which sermons are delivered, was added near the mihrab. These modifications ensured that Hagia Sophia remained a central place of worship and a symbol of Islamic power and culture throughout the Ottoman era.

The architectural blend of Byzantine and Ottoman elements makes Hagia Sophia unique. The addition of minarets and other Islamic features created a harmonious fusion of Christian and Islamic architecture, reflecting the complex history and cultural interactions of the region. The building continued to serve as a mosque until 1935, when Mustafa Kemal Atatürk, the founder of modern Turkey, secularized Hagia Sophia and transformed it into a museum. This decision was part of a broader effort to modernize and secularize Turkey, and it allowed for the preservation and study of the building's rich historical and artistic heritage.

As a museum, Hagia Sophia attracted millions of visitors from around the world, who came to admire its architectural beauty, historical significance, and artistic treasures. The process of uncovering and restoring the mosaics that had been plastered over during the Ottoman period revealed the stunning artistry of the Byzantine era and provided invaluable insights into the cultural and religious life of Constantinople.

In recent years, Hagia Sophia's status has been the subject of renewed debate and controversy. In 2020, the Turkish government, led by President Recep Tayyip Erdoğan, decided to reconvert Hagia Sophia into a mosque, a move that sparked both domestic and international reactions. The decision was seen by some as a reaffirmation of Turkey's Islamic heritage, while others viewed it as a step back from the secular principles established by Atatürk. Despite its reconversion to a mosque, Hagia Sophia remains open to visitors, continuing to serve as a symbol of the country's rich and diverse history.

The architectural and historical significance of Hagia Sophia extends beyond its religious functions. The building has influenced architectural design and engineering throughout history, serving as a model for numerous other religious and secular buildings. The Hagia Sophia's dome, in particular, has inspired architects across different cultures and periods, including the designers of the famous Blue Mosque in Istanbul and St. Peter's Basilica in Vatican City.

Hagia Sophia also holds a special place in the cultural and intellectual history of the Byzantine and Ottoman empires. It was not only a center of religious life but also a hub of intellectual and artistic activity. During the Byzantine period, it was the site of significant theological debates and ecclesiastical councils. The building's beauty and grandeur were celebrated in contemporary literature and art, reflecting its importance as a symbol of divine wisdom and imperial power.

The continued study and preservation of Hagia Sophia are essential for understanding the complex and interwoven histories of the Byzantine and Ottoman empires, as well as the broader history of Christianity and Islam. Archaeologists, historians, and art historians have dedicated considerable effort to uncovering the layers of history embedded in the structure, revealing new insights into the technological innovations, artistic traditions, and cultural exchanges that have shaped the building over the centuries.

Chapter 17: Moai of Easter Island

The Moai of Easter Island, known as Rapa Nui to its indigenous Polynesian inhabitants, are among the most enigmatic and fascinating archaeological wonders of the world. These monolithic human figures, carved from volcanic tuff, are a testament to the ingenuity and artistry of the ancient Rapa Nui people. The Moai statues, numbering around 887, were created between the 13th and 16th centuries and are spread across the island, which lies in the southeastern Pacific Ocean, roughly 3,500 kilometers west of Chile.

The Moai are renowned for their large heads, which comprise about three-eighths of the statues' overall height. These statues, with an average height of 4 meters and weighing around 12.5 metric tons, exhibit a distinctive and stylized human form. The largest Moai, called Paro, is almost 10 meters tall and weighs 82 tons, while some unfinished statues in the quarry, such as El Gigante, are even larger, suggesting the incredible ambition and capability of their creators.

The majority of the Moai were carved from the volcanic tuff of Rano Raraku, a quarry located in the southeastern part of the island. This quarry contains numerous incomplete statues, offering insights into the carving techniques and processes used by the Rapa Nui people. The Moai were meticulously crafted using basalt stone picks and chisels, which were used to shape the statues from the relatively soft volcanic rock. The level of detail and craftsmanship in these statues is remarkable, with some featuring intricate carvings that indicate body ornaments and tattoos.

Once carved, the Moai were transported from the quarry to their intended locations on stone platforms known as ahu, which are often situated along the coast of the island. The transportation of these massive statues remains one of the most intriguing aspects of the Moai's history. Theories about how the Rapa Nui moved these colossal figures have varied over the years. Early European explorers speculated that the statues were transported using wooden sledges and rollers. However, given the limited availability of wood on the island, this theory has been largely discounted.

Recent research suggests that the Moai may have been "walked" to their destinations using a sophisticated system of ropes and human labor. This hypothesis is supported by experiments in which teams of researchers were able to move replicas of the statues in an upright position by rocking them from side to side while coordinating their efforts with ropes. This method, which would have required considerable coordination and strength, aligns with oral traditions of the Rapa Nui that describe the statues as having "walked" to their locations.

The placement of the Moai on the ahu was a deeply significant act, imbued with religious and social meaning. The Moai were erected to honor important ancestors and were believed to embody their mana, or spiritual power. Positioned to face inland, the statues watched over the villages and protected the inhabitants. This placement underscored the Moai's role as intermediaries between the human world and the spiritual realm, reinforcing social cohesion and continuity.

The construction of the ahu platforms was an equally impressive feat of engineering. These platforms were built using large, finely fitted stones and often featured a ramp leading up to the base of the Moai. The ahu also served as burial sites, with some containing the remains of high-status individuals. The alignment and construction of the ahu reflect the sophisticated understanding of astronomy and geometry possessed by the Rapa Nui.

One of the most famous sites on Easter Island is Ahu Tongariki, the largest ahu on the island, which once supported 15 Moai. This site was partially destroyed by a tsunami in 1960, but subsequent restoration efforts have returned the Moai to their original positions, showcasing the grandeur and scale of the site. Ahu Tongariki provides a vivid illustration of the Rapa Nui's ability to organize and mobilize large groups of people to achieve monumental construction projects.

Despite their impressive achievements, the Rapa Nui faced significant challenges, particularly in terms of environmental sustainability. Deforestation, driven by the need for timber and agricultural expansion, led to soil erosion and a decline in the island's ability to support its population. This environmental degradation, combined with social and political strife, likely contributed to the eventual decline of the Moai-building culture. By the time European explorers arrived in the 18th century, the society that had created these remarkable statues had undergone significant changes, and many Moai had been toppled.

The reasons for the toppling of the Moai remain a subject of debate among researchers. Some suggest that the statues were deliberately knocked down during periods of social conflict and upheaval. Others propose that natural disasters, such as earthquakes, may have contributed to their collapse. Regardless of the cause, the fallen Moai symbolize the dramatic transformations and challenges faced by the Rapa Nui society.

The arrival of European explorers, beginning with the Dutch expedition led by Jacob Roggeveen in 1722, marked the beginning of a new chapter in the island's history. European contact brought new diseases, which, along with the island's existing environmental challenges, had a devastating impact on the Rapa Nui population. The introduction of the slave trade in the 19th century further exacerbated these issues, leading to significant depopulation and cultural disruption.

In the 20th century, interest in the Moai and the history of Easter Island led to numerous archaeological studies and restoration projects. Researchers have worked to understand the cultural and historical context of the Moai, uncovering insights into the social organization, religious beliefs, and technological capabilities of the Rapa Nui.

Restoration efforts have aimed to preserve the Moai and their ahu, protecting them from the effects of weathering and human activity.

Today, Easter Island is a UNESCO World Heritage Site, and the Moai continue to captivate the imagination of people around the world. The island's remote location, combined with its rich cultural heritage, makes it a unique destination for scholars, tourists, and those interested in the mysteries of the past. The preservation and study of the Moai provide valuable insights into the resilience and creativity of the Rapa Nui people, offering lessons on the importance of sustainable resource management and the enduring impact of cultural heritage.

Chapter 18: The Pantheon

The Pantheon, located in the heart of Rome, Italy, is one of the most well-preserved and architecturally significant buildings from the ancient world. Originally built as a temple for all the Roman gods, the Pantheon has stood the test of time, serving various purposes throughout its nearly 2,000-year history. Its impressive dome, innovative design, and historical significance make the Pantheon a subject of endless fascination and admiration.

The original Pantheon was commissioned by Marcus Agrippa during the reign of Augustus (27 BCE – 14 CE). This first structure, however, was destroyed by fire in 80 CE. The current Pantheon, which we see today, was rebuilt by the Emperor Hadrian around 118-125 CE. Hadrian's Pantheon was dedicated in 126 CE, and it has since been in continuous use. Despite numerous modifications and restorations over the centuries, the building has retained much of its original grandeur and design.

The Pantheon's architecture is a masterpiece of Roman engineering. The building's most distinctive feature is its massive domed roof, which remains the largest unreinforced concrete dome in the world. The dome is a perfect hemisphere, measuring 43.3 meters (142 feet) in diameter, which is exactly the same as its height from the floor to the oculus. This symmetry creates a sense of balance and harmony within the space. The dome's thickness gradually decreases as it rises, from 6.4 meters (21 feet) at the base to 1.2 meters (4 feet) at the oculus, demonstrating the Romans' advanced understanding of engineering and materials.

The oculus, a 9-meter (30-foot) wide circular opening at the apex of the dome, is the Pantheon's only source of natural light. It serves both a practical and symbolic purpose. Practically, it provides illumination to the interior space, creating a dramatic effect as the sunlight moves across the floor and walls. Symbolically, the oculus represents the all-seeing eye of heaven, connecting the temple to the divine. The oculus also serves as a natural ventilation system, allowing rainwater to enter the building but also to be efficiently drained away through a series of holes in the floor.

The Pantheon's portico, or entrance, is equally impressive. It features a rectangular colonnade with eight Corinthian columns at the front and two rows of four columns behind, made of Egyptian granite with bases and capitals of white Greek marble. The columns support a triangular pediment, which originally would have been adorned with a sculptural relief. The portico leads into a large, circular interior space, known as the rotunda, which is capped by the dome. The transition from the portico to the rotunda is mediated by a massive bronze door, which, although not original, dates back to ancient times and adds to the building's historical aura.

Inside, the Pantheon's interior is a marvel of spatial design and decorative opulence. The floor is laid out in a geometric pattern of squares and circles, made from a variety of colorful marbles sourced from across the Roman Empire. This elaborate flooring adds to the visual complexity and richness of the space. The walls of the rotunda are divided into a series of recessed panels, or coffers, which not only add to the aesthetic appeal but also reduce the weight of the dome. Originally, these coffers would have been adorned with gilded bronze rosettes, further enhancing the splendor of the interior.

The Pantheon's interior also features a series of niches and altars, originally designed to hold statues of the Roman gods. There are seven large niches, one of which, directly opposite the entrance, forms a semi-circular apse. This layout reflects the Pantheon's original function as a temple to all the gods, with each niche likely dedicated to a specific deity. Over time, these niches have been repurposed to accommodate Christian altars and monuments, reflecting the building's conversion to a Christian church in the early 7th century.

The Pantheon was consecrated as a Christian church in 609 CE by Pope Boniface IV, who dedicated it to St. Mary and the Martyrs, thereby ensuring its preservation through the centuries. This conversion helped protect the building from the widespread destruction that befell many ancient Roman structures during the Middle Ages. As a church, the Pantheon continued to be an important religious site and became a popular place for Christian burials.

One of the most famous individuals interred in the Pantheon is the Renaissance artist Raphael, whose tomb is located in a niche on the left side of the entrance. Raphael's epitaph, written by the poet Pietro Bembo, honors the artist's contributions to art and his enduring legacy. The Pantheon also houses the tombs of several Italian kings, including Victor Emmanuel II, the first king of unified Italy, and his successor, Umberto I, along with Umberto's queen, Margherita of Savoy.

Throughout its history, the Pantheon has undergone several restorations and modifications. In the early 17th century, Pope Urban VIII ordered the removal of the bronze from the portico's beams, which was used to create the baldachin over the altar in St. Peter's Basilica and to cast cannon for the Castel Sant'Angelo. Despite this, the Pantheon has largely retained its original architectural integrity and continues to be a source of inspiration for architects and artists.

The Pantheon's influence on architecture is profound and far-reaching. Its innovative design and engineering have inspired countless buildings throughout history, particularly during the Renaissance and the Neoclassical period. The use of the dome, in particular, became a defining feature of many important structures, such as the Florence Cathedral, St. Peter's Basilica in Rome, and the United States Capitol in Washington, D.C. The Pantheon's harmonious proportions, structural ingenuity, and aesthetic beauty have made it a timeless model of architectural excellence.

In addition to its architectural significance, the Pantheon holds an important place in the cultural and religious history of Rome. It stands as a testament to the city's rich and layered history, from its origins in the Roman Empire to its transformation into a center of Christian worship. The building's ability to adapt and endure through centuries of change is a testament to the resilience and continuity of Rome itself.

The Pantheon's continued use as a church and tourist attraction ensures that it remains a living monument, bridging the past and the present. Visitors from around the world come to admire its architectural splendor, reflect on its historical significance, and experience the unique atmosphere created by its magnificent interior. The building's preservation and conservation are ongoing concerns, as efforts are made to protect it from the effects of pollution, weathering, and the wear and tear of millions of visitors.

Chapter 19: Gobekli Tepe

Göbekli Tepe, located in southeastern Turkey, is one of the most extraordinary and significant archaeological discoveries of the late 20th century. This ancient site, dating back to the Pre-Pottery Neolithic period (circa 9600 to 8200 BCE), challenges many conventional theories about the development of human societies and the origins of complex social structures. The site consists of a series of monumental stone circles, featuring massive T-shaped pillars adorned with intricate carvings, making Göbekli Tepe the world's oldest known temple complex and a pivotal point in our understanding of prehistoric human culture.

The discovery of Göbekli Tepe was made in the mid-1960s, but it wasn't until the mid-1990s that Klaus Schmidt, a German archaeologist, began extensive excavations that brought its significance to light. The site, located on a hilltop near the city of Şanlıurfa, covers an area of about 300 meters in diameter. Göbekli Tepe consists of numerous circular and oval-shaped structures, with some of the most prominent features being the large T-shaped limestone pillars, which stand up to 5.5 meters tall and weigh as much as 10 tons. These pillars are arranged in a series of concentric circles, with two larger central pillars surrounded by smaller ones.

The intricate carvings on the pillars are among the most remarkable aspects of Göbekli Tepe. These carvings include depictions of animals such as lions, bulls, snakes, foxes, and birds, as well as abstract symbols and human-like figures. The detailed and varied iconography suggests that the builders of Göbekli Tepe had a rich symbolic and spiritual life, with the carvings likely representing deities, mythological figures, or totemic animals. The craftsmanship of these carvings indicates a high level of skill and artistry, challenging previous assumptions about the capabilities of early Neolithic societies.

One of the most intriguing aspects of Göbekli Tepe is its purpose. The lack of domestic structures and the presence of monumental architecture suggest that it was a site of significant ritual and ceremonial activity, rather than a settlement for everyday living. This challenges the conventional narrative that complex social and religious structures emerged only after the development of agriculture and settled communities. Instead, Göbekli Tepe implies that complex spiritual practices and the construction of monumental architecture may have preceded and even facilitated the transition to agricultural societies.

The construction of Göbekli Tepe would have required a considerable amount of labor and coordination, indicating a high degree of social organization. The site's builders likely had to quarry, transport, and erect the massive stone pillars, a task that would have required the cooperation of a large group of people. This level of organization suggests that early human societies were capable of complex collective activities long before the advent of permanent settlements and agriculture.

The site also provides valuable insights into the symbolic and ritual practices of early human societies. The arrangement of the pillars in circular formations, along with the central positioning of the larger pillars, suggests that the structures may have been used for communal gatherings, rituals, or ceremonies. The carvings on the pillars could represent protective spirits or deities, and their positioning within the circles may have had cosmological or spiritual significance. The emphasis on animal imagery also suggests a close connection between the inhabitants of Göbekli Tepe and the natural world, with animals playing a central role in their symbolic and ritual life.

Göbekli Tepe's significance extends beyond its architectural and artistic achievements. The site also provides crucial evidence about the transition from hunter-gatherer societies to agricultural ones. While the builders of Göbekli Tepe were primarily hunter-gatherers, the need to sustain a large labor force for the construction and maintenance of the site may have contributed to the domestication of plants and animals. This process, in turn, could have led to the development of more permanent settlements and the eventual rise of agriculture.

The excavation and study of Göbekli Tepe have also revealed important information about the diet and subsistence practices of its builders. Archaeobotanical and zooarchaeological analyses have shown that the people of Göbekli Tepe consumed a diverse range of wild plants and animals, including einkorn wheat, barley, pistachios, wild boar, deer, and various bird species. The presence of grinding stones and other tools suggests that they processed plant foods, indicating a sophisticated knowledge of plant resources. The combination of hunting, gathering, and possibly early forms of plant cultivation highlights the diverse subsistence strategies employed by the site's inhabitants.

Another fascinating aspect of Göbekli Tepe is its deliberate burial under tons of soil and rubble around 8,000 BCE. The reasons for this intentional act remain a subject of speculation and debate among archaeologists. Some theories suggest that the site's burial was part of a ritual practice, possibly to mark the end of its use as a ceremonial center. Others propose that the burial was a way to preserve the site for future generations or to protect it from potential threats. Regardless of the reason, the burial of Göbekli Tepe has contributed to its remarkable state of preservation, allowing archaeologists to study its structures and carvings in great detail.

Göbekli Tepe's discovery and subsequent research have had a profound impact on our understanding of prehistoric human societies. The site challenges long-held assumptions about the development of complex social structures, the role of religion in early human communities, and the origins of monumental architecture. It suggests that the impetus for building large, communal structures may have been driven by spiritual and ritual needs rather than purely economic or practical considerations. This, in turn, has implications for our understanding of the factors that led to the rise of agriculture and settled societies.

The study of Göbekli Tepe also highlights the importance of symbolic and ritual behavior in early human societies. The site's intricate carvings and monumental architecture reflect a rich symbolic life and suggest that the builders had complex beliefs and practices. This challenges the notion that early human societies were primarily focused on survival and subsistence and instead emphasizes the central role of symbolic and ritual behavior in human history.

Göbekli Tepe continues to be a focus of intense archaeological research and interest. Ongoing excavations and studies aim to uncover more about the site's construction, use, and significance. Researchers are also exploring the broader landscape around Göbekli Tepe, seeking to understand its relationship with other contemporary sites and its place within the wider context of early Neolithic developments in the region.

In addition to its archaeological significance, Göbekli Tepe has also become an important cultural and heritage site. It was inscribed as a UNESCO World Heritage Site in 2018, recognizing its outstanding universal value and the need to preserve and protect it for future generations. Efforts are underway to ensure the site's conservation and to manage the impact of tourism, which has increased significantly since its discovery.

Chapter 20: Borobudur

Borobudur is a colossal Buddhist monument in Central Java, Indonesia, widely regarded as one of the greatest Buddhist monuments in the world. Built in the 9th century during the reign of the Sailendra Dynasty, Borobudur is an architectural and cultural marvel that has fascinated historians, archaeologists, and travelers for centuries. The monument is a vast, tiered structure, built in the form of a step pyramid, consisting of nine stacked platforms, six square and three circular, topped by a central dome. The entire structure is adorned with 2,672 relief panels and 504 Buddha statues, creating a symphony of art, religion, and architecture.

The origin of Borobudur is shrouded in mystery, with no written records detailing its construction or purpose. It is believed to have been commissioned by King Samaratungga of the Sailendra Dynasty, who ruled over Java during a period of great religious and cultural flowering. The construction of Borobudur took approximately 75 years to complete and was finished around 825 CE. The name 'Borobudur' is thought to derive from the Sanskrit words 'Vihara Buddha Uhr,' which roughly translates to 'the Buddhist monastery on the hill.'

Borobudur is designed as a mandala, which is a spiritual and ritual symbol in Hinduism and Buddhism representing the universe. The monument's architecture symbolizes the stages of enlightenment in Buddhist cosmology. The base of the monument represents Kamadhatu, the world of desires, where human beings are bound by their physical and earthly cravings. The relief panels on this level depict scenes from human life, illustrating moral stories that guide individuals toward the path of righteousness.

Above Kamadhatu are the five square platforms representing Rupadhatu, the world of forms, where humans transcend earthly desires but are still bound by name and form. The relief panels on these levels depict various stories from the life of the Buddha and Jataka tales, which are stories of the Buddha's previous lives. These intricate carvings are not only artistic masterpieces but also serve as didactic tools, teaching the principles of Buddhism through visual storytelling.

The upper three circular platforms represent Arupadhatu, the formless world, where physical and mental forms cease to exist, and one attains nirvana. These levels are adorned with 72 stupas, each containing a statue of the Buddha in a meditation pose, symbolizing the state of ultimate enlightenment. The central dome at the top of the monument represents the achievement of enlightenment itself, the ultimate goal in Buddhism.

Borobudur's construction is an engineering marvel. The entire structure is made of andesite stone, and it was built without the use of mortar. The stones were cut to fit precisely together, and interlocking designs were used to ensure the stability of the monument. The monument's drainage system is a testament to the advanced engineering skills of its builders, with a series of hidden channels and spouts preventing water damage to the structure during heavy rains.

The discovery of Borobudur in the 19th century is a story of rediscovery and restoration. The monument was abandoned in the 14th century, likely due to the decline of Buddhist and Hindu kingdoms in Java and the rise of Islam. Over the centuries, it was buried under layers of volcanic ash and jungle growth, forgotten by the local population. In 1814, Sir Thomas Stamford Raffles, the British Governor of Java, was informed of its existence by local residents. He initiated a survey and clearing of the site, unveiling the magnificent structure hidden beneath the jungle.

In the 20th century, Borobudur underwent several restoration efforts to preserve its grandeur. The most significant restoration project took place between 1975 and 1982, led by the Indonesian government and UNESCO. This massive undertaking involved dismantling and rebuilding parts of the monument, cleaning the stone surfaces, and improving the drainage system to ensure the long-term preservation of Borobudur. The restoration efforts were a testament to the global recognition of Borobudur's cultural and historical significance.

Today, Borobudur is a UNESCO World Heritage Site and one of Indonesia's most visited tourist attractions. It remains a place of pilgrimage for Buddhists from around the world, especially during Vesak, an important Buddhist festival that celebrates the birth, enlightenment, and death of the Buddha. The monument's serene and majestic presence amidst the lush Javanese landscape continues to inspire awe and reverence in all who visit.

Borobudur is not only an architectural wonder but also a symbol of Indonesia's rich cultural heritage. It reflects the profound spiritual and artistic achievements of the ancient Javanese civilization. The monument's intricate carvings and statues offer a glimpse into the religious and philosophical thought of the time, showcasing the syncretic nature of Javanese culture, which integrated elements of Buddhism, Hinduism, and indigenous beliefs.

In recent years, Borobudur has faced challenges due to environmental and human factors. Volcanic eruptions, earthquakes, and climate change pose threats to its structural integrity, while the growing number of tourists raises concerns about conservation and sustainability. Efforts are ongoing to balance the preservation of this ancient monument with the demands of modern tourism, ensuring that future generations can continue to marvel at Borobudur's timeless beauty and spiritual significance.

Chapter 21: The Terracotta Army

The Terracotta Army is one of the most significant archaeological discoveries of the 20th century and a profound testament to the power and ambition of China's first emperor, Qin Shi Huang. Discovered in 1974 by local farmers near the city of Xi'an in Shaanxi Province, this vast collection of terracotta sculptures represents the armies of Qin Shi Huang, who unified China in 221 BCE and became its first emperor. The Terracotta Army was created to protect the emperor in the afterlife, reflecting the ancient Chinese belief in life after death and the need to safeguard one's status and power beyond the mortal realm.

The army is part of a much larger necropolis, which covers an area of about 98 square kilometers. The central tomb itself remains unexcavated due to concerns over preserving the artifacts and potential dangers, such as high levels of mercury, which ancient texts suggest were used to simulate rivers and seas within the tomb. The terracotta soldiers were found in three main pits, which are situated about 1.5 kilometers east of the emperor's tomb mound. Each pit contains a unique arrangement of figures, chariots, and horses, meticulously arranged to replicate a real military formation.

Pit 1 is the largest and most impressive, measuring approximately 230 meters long and 62 meters wide. It contains an estimated 6,000 figures, including infantry, chariots, and cavalry, arranged in a rectangular formation. The soldiers are organized in precise rows, with chariots at the front, followed by infantry in the center and cavalry on the flanks. This pit alone gives a sense of the scale and complexity of the Terracotta Army, reflecting the highly organized and hierarchical nature of Qin Shi Huang's military forces.

Pit 2, slightly smaller, contains a more diverse array of military units, including archers, crossbowmen, and cavalry. It is believed to represent the vanguard of the army, with the soldiers poised in dynamic stances, ready for battle. The figures in this pit showcase the skill and artistry of the craftsmen who created them, as each figure is uniquely detailed, with distinct facial features, hairstyles, and expressions. The meticulous attention to detail extends to the weapons and armor, which were made of bronze and were fully functional, further emphasizing the realistic representation of the emperor's army.

Pit 3, the smallest of the three, is thought to be the command center of the army. It contains high-ranking officers and chariots, symbolizing the strategic and leadership elements of the military formation. The figures in this pit are fewer in number but no less impressive in their craftsmanship and detail. The layout and contents of Pit 3 suggest a well-organized and highly structured command hierarchy, mirroring the organizational principles that underpinned Qin Shi Huang's empire.

The construction of the Terracotta Army involved the labor of thousands of artisans and workers over several decades. The figures were crafted using a combination of assembly line techniques and individual artistry. The bodies were mass-produced in molds, while the heads, arms, and hands were individually sculpted and attached, allowing for a remarkable degree of individuality among the figures. This method ensured both efficiency in production and a unique identity for each soldier, reflecting the diverse makeup of Qin Shi Huang's army.

The terracotta figures were originally painted in vibrant colors, including red, blue, green, and gold, adding to their lifelike appearance. However, exposure to air and moisture after their excavation caused the paint to flake off, leaving the figures with their now-familiar terracotta hue. Efforts are ongoing to preserve and restore the original colors, using advanced technologies and techniques to stabilize and protect the fragile pigments.

In addition to the soldiers, the Terracotta Army complex includes a variety of other figures and artifacts, such as acrobats, musicians, and officials, representing the broader aspects of court life and the emperor's desire to recreate his world in the afterlife. These ancillary figures provide valuable insights into the culture, society, and daily life of the Qin Dynasty, offering a more comprehensive understanding of the period.

The discovery of the Terracotta Army has greatly enhanced our knowledge of ancient Chinese history, particularly the Qin Dynasty and the reign of Qin Shi Huang. The army not only reflects the military prowess and organizational skills of the emperor but also his innovative spirit and vision for a unified China. Qin Shi Huang is credited with numerous reforms and achievements, including the standardization of weights and measures, the creation of a uniform writing system, and the construction of major infrastructure projects such as roads and canals.

The Terracotta Army also underscores the emperor's belief in the afterlife and his efforts to secure his legacy and protection beyond death. The scale and intricacy of the necropolis reflect the immense resources and manpower that were mobilized for its construction, highlighting the centralized power and control exercised by Qin Shi Huang. The project would have required not only a vast workforce but also skilled artisans, engineers, and planners, demonstrating the advanced state of technology and organization during the period.

Since their discovery, the terracotta figures have become a symbol of China's rich cultural heritage and have attracted millions of visitors from around the world. The site has been designated a UNESCO World Heritage Site, recognizing its outstanding historical and cultural significance. Ongoing archaeological work continues to uncover new findings, adding to our understanding of this extraordinary monument and the civilization that created it.

The Terracotta Army has also had a profound impact on popular culture, inspiring numerous books, films, and exhibitions. Its influence extends beyond China, resonating with audiences globally and sparking interest in ancient Chinese history and archaeology. The figures' lifelike appearance and the sheer scale of the army evoke a sense of awe and wonder, drawing people into the story of Qin Shi Huang and his monumental legacy.

Chapter 22: Tikal

Tikal, one of the largest and most important archaeological sites of the ancient Maya civilization, is situated in the rainforests of northern Guatemala. This UNESCO World Heritage site was once a major city and a cultural, political, and economic hub of the Maya world. Tikal's history spans several centuries, peaking during the Classic Period from approximately 200 to 900 CE. The site covers around 16 square kilometers, with thousands of structures, including temples, palaces, ceremonial platforms, plazas, and residential areas. The grandeur and complexity of Tikal provide invaluable insights into the Maya civilization, its architectural prowess, societal structure, and cultural achievements.

The origins of Tikal date back to the Preclassic Period, around 600 BCE, when the first settlers began to establish the city. By the Late Preclassic Period (300 BCE - 250 CE), Tikal had grown into a significant urban center. The city's development accelerated during the Early Classic Period (250 - 600 CE), marked by the construction of monumental architecture and the establishment of Tikal as a dominant force in the region. The city's rulers, known as ajaw or kings, played a crucial role in its expansion, engaging in warfare, diplomacy, and trade to extend Tikal's influence.

One of the most striking features of Tikal is its towering pyramidal temples. The Great Plaza, the heart of Tikal, is flanked by two of these impressive structures: Temple I (also known as the Temple of the Great Jaguar) and Temple II (the Temple of the Masks). Temple I, rising to a height of 47 meters, was constructed during the reign of Jasaw Chan K'awiil I in the 8th century. It served as both a funerary monument and a symbol of the king's power. The temple's steep stairs lead to a small summit shrine, where important rituals and ceremonies were performed. Temple II, slightly smaller at 38 meters, was built by Jasaw Chan K'awiil I to honor his wife, Lady Kalajuun Une' Mo'.

The two temples face each other across the Great Plaza, reflecting the architectural and ceremonial sophistication of the Maya.

The North Acropolis, located adjacent to the Great Plaza, is another significant complex in Tikal. This acropolis served as a royal necropolis, housing the tombs of several prominent rulers. The North Acropolis evolved over centuries, with successive layers of construction reflecting the city's changing political and religious landscape. The intricate carvings and hieroglyphic inscriptions on the stelae and altars found here provide valuable information about Tikal's rulers, their achievements, and their lineage.

Tikal's Central Acropolis, a sprawling complex of interconnected palaces and courtyards, highlights the city's political and administrative functions. This area likely served as the residence for the elite and administrative officials, as well as the site for important governmental activities. The layout of the Central Acropolis, with its multi-story structures and labyrinthine corridors, demonstrates advanced architectural and engineering skills. The construction techniques employed by the Maya, such as corbelled vaults and buttressed walls, allowed for the creation of large, stable buildings capable of withstanding the test of time.

Another notable feature of Tikal is its extensive network of causeways, known as sacbeob. These elevated roads connected various parts of the city and its outlying areas, facilitating the movement of people and goods. The sacbeob were not only practical infrastructure but also had symbolic significance, representing the pathways of the gods and the connections between different realms of the Maya cosmology. The presence of these causeways underscores the importance of trade and communication in sustaining Tikal's growth and influence.

Tikal's decline began in the late 9th century, coinciding with the broader collapse of the Classic Maya civilization. The reasons for this decline are complex and multifaceted, likely involving a combination of environmental factors, resource depletion, social upheaval, and external pressures from rival city-states. By the end of the 10th century, Tikal was largely abandoned, its monumental structures gradually reclaimed by the surrounding jungle. Despite its decline, Tikal's legacy endured through its architectural achievements, cultural contributions, and the historical records inscribed on its monuments.

The rediscovery of Tikal in the 19th century by European explorers brought the ancient city back into the spotlight. Early explorations by individuals such as Modesto Méndez and Ambrosio Tut, who documented the site in the 1840s, laid the groundwork for future archaeological investigations. Subsequent expeditions, particularly those led by institutions like the University of Pennsylvania and the Guatemalan government in the mid-20th century, undertook extensive excavations and restorations. These efforts have uncovered a wealth of information about Tikal's history, architecture, and society, contributing significantly to our understanding of the Maya civilization.

Tikal's significance extends beyond its architectural and historical importance. The site is also a vital part of the natural environment, situated within the Tikal National Park, a protected area of tropical rainforest. The park is home to a diverse array of flora and fauna, including endangered species such as jaguars, howler monkeys, and numerous bird species. The coexistence of the archaeological site and its surrounding ecosystem highlights the ancient Maya's connection to their environment and the need for modern conservation efforts to preserve both cultural heritage and biodiversity.

In recent years, advances in technology, such as LiDAR (Light Detection and Ranging), have revolutionized the study of Tikal and other Maya sites. LiDAR surveys have revealed previously hidden structures and features beneath the dense jungle canopy, providing new insights into the scale and complexity of the city. These discoveries have challenged previous assumptions about Maya urbanism, suggesting that Tikal was part of an extensive network of interconnected settlements, with a higher population density and more sophisticated infrastructure than previously thought.

The cultural and historical legacy of Tikal continues to captivate scholars and visitors alike. The site's intricate carvings, towering temples, and mysterious origins offer a glimpse into the achievements and challenges of one of the ancient world's most advanced civilizations. As research and conservation efforts continue, Tikal remains a focal point for understanding the Maya civilization, its contributions to human history, and the lessons it offers for contemporary societies.

Tikal is not just an ancient city frozen in time; it is a dynamic testament to human ingenuity, resilience, and the enduring quest for knowledge and meaning. Its towering temples and sprawling complexes stand as silent witnesses to the rise and fall of a great civilization, while its jungles pulse with the life that once thrived in harmony with its human inhabitants. Through ongoing study and preservation, Tikal will continue to reveal its secrets and inspire future generations to explore and cherish our shared heritage.

Chapter 23: Tower of Babel

The Tower of Babel, a biblical structure mentioned in Genesis 11:1-9, is one of the most famous and enigmatic edifices in human history. It has captured the imagination of countless generations with its tale of human ambition, divine intervention, and linguistic diversity. The story begins after the Great Flood, when humanity, unified by a single language, settled in the land of Shinar, believed to be in Mesopotamia, present-day Iraq. The people, seeking to make a name for themselves and avoid being scattered across the earth, decided to build a city and a tower "with its top in the heavens."

The construction of the Tower of Babel was a monumental undertaking, symbolizing human ingenuity and cooperation. The builders used baked bricks and bitumen for mortar, materials that were abundant in Mesopotamia and ideal for large-scale construction. The choice of these materials reflects the technological advancements of the time, showcasing the ability to produce durable and uniform building blocks. The use of bitumen, a natural asphalt, for mortar further indicates an understanding of engineering principles necessary for constructing a tall and stable structure.

As the tower rose towards the heavens, it became a symbol of human pride and defiance against divine authority. The ambition to build a tower that reached the heavens can be interpreted as an attempt to challenge God's supremacy and establish human dominance. This act of hubris did not go unnoticed by God, who decided to intervene to halt the construction. According to the biblical account, God confused the language of the people, causing them to speak different languages and thus making it impossible for them to understand each other. This confusion led to the cessation of the construction and the scattering of humanity across the earth, giving rise to the diverse languages and cultures we see today.

The story of the Tower of Babel serves as an allegory for the limits of human ambition and the consequences of overreaching pride. It highlights the dangers of attempting to transcend human limitations and the inevitable disruption that follows when collective efforts are driven by arrogance rather than humility and reverence for higher powers. The narrative also underscores the importance of communication and cooperation in achieving common goals. The confusion of languages symbolizes the breakdown of these essential elements, resulting in division and dispersal.

Beyond its biblical context, the Tower of Babel has influenced various cultural, literary, and artistic expressions throughout history. In medieval Christian thought, it was often depicted as a cautionary tale against the sin of pride, with numerous paintings, sculptures, and manuscripts illustrating the dramatic moment when the builders were struck by divine confusion. Artists like Pieter Bruegel the Elder and Gustave Doré created iconic images of the tower, capturing its imposing structure and the chaos that ensued among the builders.

The Tower of Babel has also inspired numerous interpretations and adaptations in literature. Writers such as John Milton, in his epic poem "Paradise Lost," and Jorge Luis Borges, in his short story "The Library of Babel," explored themes of human ambition, divine retribution, and the quest for knowledge through the lens of the Babel narrative. These literary works delve into the complexities of the human condition, reflecting on the interplay between aspiration and limitation, unity and fragmentation.

In the field of linguistics, the story of the Tower of Babel has been used metaphorically to describe the diversity of languages and the challenges of communication across different linguistic and cultural boundaries. The term "Babel" has become synonymous with confusion and miscommunication, often invoked in discussions about the difficulties of achieving mutual understanding in a multilingual world.

The story underscores the significance of language as both a unifying and divisive force, shaping human interactions and societal structures.

Archaeologically, the historical basis for the Tower of Babel has been a topic of debate and speculation. Some scholars have suggested that the tower might be inspired by real ziggurats, which were massive stepped structures built in ancient Mesopotamia as temples to the gods. The most famous of these is the Etemenanki, dedicated to the god Marduk in the city of Babylon. Etemenanki, meaning "House of the Foundation of Heaven and Earth," was an enormous ziggurat that stood approximately 91 meters tall. Its grandeur and prominence could have inspired the biblical account of the Tower of Babel, serving as a tangible representation of humanity's reach for the divine.

Historical records, such as those from Herodotus and other ancient historians, describe Babylon as a city of immense wealth and architectural splendor, with towering structures that reached towards the skies. These descriptions, coupled with archaeological evidence, lend credence to the idea that the biblical Tower of Babel may have been based on these grand Mesopotamian ziggurats. The construction techniques, materials used, and the sheer scale of these structures demonstrate the advanced engineering capabilities of ancient civilizations and their aspirations to connect with the divine.

In modern times, the Tower of Babel continues to resonate as a powerful symbol in various fields, including architecture, philosophy, and technology. In architecture, it represents the challenges and aspirations associated with building monumental structures. The drive to construct skyscrapers and other towering edifices in contemporary cities can be seen as a reflection of humanity's enduring desire to reach new heights and assert its presence in the world. The story of Babel serves as a reminder of the balance that must be struck between ambition and humility, innovation and respect for natural and divine limits.

Philosophically, the Tower of Babel raises questions about the nature of human progress, the pursuit of knowledge, and the consequences of technological advancement. It prompts reflection on the ethical and moral implications of pushing boundaries and the potential for unintended consequences when humanity seeks to surpass its limits. The narrative encourages a critical examination of the motivations driving human endeavors and the importance of maintaining a sense of humility and responsibility in the face of extraordinary achievements.

In the realm of technology, the Tower of Babel metaphor is often invoked in discussions about the complexities and challenges of global communication networks. The proliferation of digital technologies and the internet has created unprecedented opportunities for connectivity and information exchange, but it has also introduced new forms of fragmentation and miscommunication. The story of Babel highlights the dual-edged nature of technological progress, where the potential for unity and understanding exists alongside the risk of division and confusion.

The Tower of Babel remains a multifaceted symbol with enduring relevance across different cultures, disciplines, and historical periods. Its themes of ambition, pride, communication, and divine intervention continue to inspire reflection and exploration. Whether viewed through the lens of theology, literature, art, linguistics, archaeology, or contemporary society, the Tower of Babel offers a rich tapestry of meanings and interpretations that illuminate the complexities of the human experience and the enduring quest for transcendence and understanding.

Chapter 24: Ajanta Caves

The Ajanta Caves, located in the Aurangabad district of Maharashtra, India, are a series of 30 rock-cut Buddhist cave monuments dating from the 2nd century BCE to about 480 CE. They are renowned for their magnificent paintings, sculptures, and architecture, representing the pinnacle of Indian rock-cut architecture and Buddhist art. The caves were rediscovered in 1819 by a British officer named John Smith, during a tiger hunting expedition, bringing to light one of the most significant archaeological finds in India.

The caves are situated in a horseshoe-shaped ravine along the Waghora River, and they are divided into two distinct groups based on their period of construction. The earlier group, attributed to the Hinayana phase of Buddhism, dates back to around the 2nd century BCE to the 1st century CE. The later group, associated with the Mahayana phase, spans from the 5th century CE onwards. This chronological division reflects the evolution of Buddhist religious practices and the development of rock-cut architecture and art over several centuries.

The Hinayana or Theravada phase of Ajanta is represented by simpler, more austere structures. Caves from this period, such as Cave 9 and Cave 10, primarily served as chaityas (prayer halls) and viharas (monastic residences). The chaityas are characterized by their horseshoe-shaped windows, known as chaitya arches, which allow natural light to illuminate the interior. Cave 9 is one of the earliest chaitya halls at Ajanta, featuring a stupa at the far end, which served as a focal point for worship. The hall is lined with columns, and the ceiling is vaulted, mimicking the form of early wooden structures.

Cave 10, another prominent chaitya hall from the Hinayana phase, is larger and more elaborately decorated. It contains an impressive array of rock-cut stupas and columns adorned with simple carvings. The hall's main feature is the large stupa at its rear end, which symbolizes the Buddha's presence. The relatively plain and unadorned style of these early caves reflects the Theravada emphasis on simplicity and meditation.

The transition to the Mahayana phase of Buddhism, starting in the 5th century CE, brought significant changes to the architectural and artistic styles of the Ajanta Caves. The Mahayana phase is characterized by more elaborate and richly decorated caves, with intricate carvings, detailed paintings, and the introduction of Buddha images. This period saw the creation of some of the most famous caves at Ajanta, including Cave 1, Cave 2, Cave 16, and Cave 17.

Cave 1 is one of the finest examples of Mahayana architecture and art at Ajanta. It is a vihara with a central hall surrounded by smaller cells for monks. The walls and ceilings are adorned with exquisite frescoes depicting scenes from the Jataka tales, which narrate the previous lives of the Buddha. The paintings in Cave 1 are renowned for their vivid colors, graceful figures, and intricate details. The most famous image in this cave is the Bodhisattva Padmapani, depicted with a serene expression, holding a lotus flower. This painting exemplifies the sophisticated artistry and spiritual depth of the Mahayana period.

Cave 2, another important Mahayana vihara, features a similar layout with a central hall and monastic cells. The walls of Cave 2 are adorned with intricate paintings that depict various episodes from the life of the Buddha, as well as scenes from the Jataka tales. The ceilings are decorated with elaborate geometric patterns and floral designs. One of the most striking features of Cave 2 is the depiction of the Thousand Buddhas, a recurring theme in Mahayana art, symbolizing the infinite manifestations of the Buddha.

Cave 16, known for its elaborate sculptures and paintings, is another highlight of the Mahayana phase at Ajanta. The entrance to the cave is adorned with intricately carved doorways and panels depicting various deities and mythological scenes. The central hall of Cave 16 contains a large statue of the Buddha in the dharmachakra mudra (the gesture of teaching), flanked by bodhisattvas and celestial beings. The walls and ceilings of the cave are covered with detailed frescoes that illustrate the Jataka tales, scenes from the Buddha's life, and other religious narratives.

Cave 17 is one of the most richly decorated caves at Ajanta, featuring a large number of well-preserved paintings. The cave is a vihara with a central hall and monastic cells, similar to other Mahayana caves. The paintings in Cave 17 are renowned for their vibrant colors, intricate details, and emotional depth. They depict a wide range of themes, including scenes from the Jataka tales, the Buddha's life, and various deities and celestial beings. The most famous painting in Cave 17 is the depiction of the Mahajanaka Jataka, which tells the story of a prince who renounces his kingdom to become a monk.

The Ajanta Caves are also notable for their sophisticated architectural techniques and engineering prowess. The caves were carved directly into the rocky cliffs using simple tools like chisels and hammers, a process that required immense skill and precision. The artisans and craftsmen who created the caves demonstrated a deep understanding of rock-cut architecture, achieving structural stability and aesthetic harmony despite the limitations of their tools and materials.

In addition to the architectural and artistic achievements, the Ajanta Caves are significant for their historical and cultural insights into the life and society of ancient India. The inscriptions and paintings in the caves provide valuable information about the patronage, social structures, and religious practices of the time. Many of the caves were commissioned by wealthy merchants, local rulers, and Buddhist monastic communities, reflecting the close relationship between religion, economy, and politics in ancient India.

The rediscovery of the Ajanta Caves in the 19th century sparked a renewed interest in Indian art and architecture, attracting scholars, artists, and travelers from around the world. The caves have since been the subject of extensive archaeological research, conservation efforts, and scholarly studies. The meticulous documentation and restoration work carried out by organizations such as the Archaeological Survey of India have helped preserve the caves and their invaluable heritage for future generations.

The Ajanta Caves continue to be a major tourist attraction and a source of inspiration for artists and scholars. The intricate carvings, vibrant paintings, and serene atmosphere of the caves offer a glimpse into the spiritual and artistic achievements of ancient India. The caves also serve as a testament to the enduring legacy of Buddhism and its profound influence on Indian culture and society.

Chapter 25: Pompeii

Pompeii, an ancient Roman city located near modern Naples in the Campania region of Italy, is one of the most significant archaeological sites in the world. Its preservation under volcanic ash provides an extraordinary snapshot of Roman life in the 1st century CE. The city met its abrupt end during the catastrophic eruption of Mount Vesuvius on August 24, 79 CE, burying it under meters of ash and pumice and preserving buildings, artifacts, and even the inhabitants in remarkable detail. This disaster, while tragic, created a time capsule that has given historians and archaeologists invaluable insights into Roman urban life, culture, and society.

The origins of Pompeii date back to around the 7th or 6th century BCE when it was founded by the Osci or Oscans, an ancient Italic people. The city later came under Greek, Etruscan, and finally Samnite influence before becoming a Roman colony in 80 BCE. As a Roman colony, Pompeii flourished, benefiting from the political stability and economic prosperity of the Roman Empire. It became a bustling city with a population estimated at about 11,000 to 15,000 inhabitants, and it was known for its thriving economy based on agriculture, trade, and industry.

The city was laid out in a typical Roman grid plan with a complex infrastructure that included streets, public buildings, private residences, shops, and entertainment venues. The Forum, the heart of Pompeii, served as the city's main public square and was surrounded by important civic buildings such as the basilica (law court), the Temple of Jupiter, and the municipal offices. The Forum was a bustling hub of social, economic, and political activity, reflecting the vibrant public life of the city.

One of the most notable aspects of Pompeii is its architecture, which showcases the ingenuity and sophistication of Roman engineering and urban planning. The city's buildings were constructed using a variety of materials, including stone, brick, and concrete, and they featured a range of architectural styles from the Italic and Hellenistic traditions to the more formal Roman styles. Public buildings, such as temples, baths, and theaters, were designed to serve the needs of the community and to reflect the grandeur of Roman culture.

The residential architecture of Pompeii is particularly remarkable for its diversity and complexity. Homes ranged from modest apartments and shops to grand villas with elaborate frescoes, mosaics, and gardens. The House of the Faun, one of the largest and most luxurious residences in Pompeii, is a prime example of Roman domestic architecture. It occupies an entire city block and features intricate floor mosaics, including the famous Alexander Mosaic, which depicts Alexander the Great's victory over Darius III at the Battle of Issus. This mosaic, with its detailed and dynamic composition, is a testament to the high level of artistry achieved by Roman craftsmen.

The House of the Vettii, another notable residence, belonged to two wealthy freedmen, Aulus Vettius Conviva and Aulus Vettius Restitutus. The house is renowned for its well-preserved frescoes, which cover the walls of its various rooms and depict scenes from mythology, daily life, and erotic imagery. The peristyle garden, an open courtyard surrounded by columns, was a central feature of the house and provided a private and serene space for relaxation and social gatherings. The decoration and layout of the House of the Vettii reflect the owners' wealth, social status, and taste.

Pompeii's public baths were another important aspect of urban life, serving as centers for social interaction, hygiene, and relaxation. The Stabian Baths, the Forum Baths, and the Central Baths are some of the well-preserved examples in the city. These bath complexes typically included a series of rooms with different temperatures: the frigidarium (cold room), tepidarium (warm room), and caldarium (hot room). The baths also featured dressing rooms, exercise areas, and sometimes libraries and gardens. The sophisticated heating system, known as the hypocaust, allowed for the efficient distribution of heat through the floors and walls, showcasing the advanced engineering skills of the Romans.

The amphitheater of Pompeii, built around 80 BCE, is one of the oldest surviving Roman amphitheaters and could accommodate up to 20,000 spectators. It was used for gladiatorial contests, animal hunts, and other forms of public entertainment. The structure of the amphitheater, with its elliptical shape and tiered seating, provided excellent visibility and acoustics for the audience. Nearby, the Palaestra, or large gymnasium, served as a training ground for athletes and a venue for various sporting activities.

The cultural life of Pompeii was rich and diverse, with influences from various parts of the Roman Empire. The city's inhabitants enjoyed a range of artistic and intellectual pursuits, as evidenced by the numerous sculptures, paintings, and inscriptions found throughout the site. The frescoes in Pompeii are particularly notable for their vibrant colors, intricate designs, and diverse themes, ranging from mythological scenes and landscapes to portraits and everyday life. These artworks provide valuable insights into the aesthetic preferences, religious beliefs, and social customs of the Pompeian people.

The economy of Pompeii was robust and multifaceted, with agriculture, trade, and industry playing key roles. The fertile volcanic soil of the region supported the cultivation of a variety of crops, including grapes, olives, and grains, which were essential to the local economy and the Mediterranean diet. Pompeii was also known for its production of wine and garum, a fermented fish sauce that was highly prized throughout the Roman Empire. The city's proximity to the Bay of Naples facilitated trade and commerce, allowing Pompeii to become a significant center for the exchange of goods and ideas.

The eruption of Mount Vesuvius in 79 CE was a catastrophic event that forever changed the course of Pompeii's history. The eruption began on August 24th and continued for approximately 18 hours, burying the city under a thick layer of volcanic ash and pumice. The suddenness of the disaster meant that many of the inhabitants were unable to escape, and their bodies were preserved in the positions in which they died, creating poignant and haunting reminders of the tragedy. The ash and pumice also encapsulated buildings, artifacts, and even the contents of homes, providing a unique and detailed snapshot of Roman life at the moment of the eruption.

The rediscovery of Pompeii in the 18th century by Spanish engineer Rocque Joaquin de Alcubierre marked the beginning of systematic archaeological excavations that have continued to the present day. These excavations have uncovered a wealth of information about the city's urban layout, architecture, and daily life. The preservation of organic materials, such as wooden furniture, food, and even graffiti, has provided an unparalleled opportunity to study the material culture of ancient Rome in detail.

One of the most striking aspects of Pompeii's preservation is the plaster casts of the victims of the eruption. In the 19th century, archaeologists developed a technique to inject plaster into the voids left by decomposed bodies in the ash layers. These casts capture the final moments of the victims, preserving their poses, expressions, and even the folds of their clothing. The casts provide a powerful and moving testament to the human cost of the disaster, bringing the people of Pompeii to life in a way that few other archaeological finds can.

The graffiti found on the walls of Pompeii offers a unique glimpse into the thoughts, humor, and daily concerns of its inhabitants. These inscriptions range from political slogans and advertisements to personal messages and jokes, revealing a vibrant and dynamic urban culture. The graffiti also includes literary quotes, love poems, and satirical comments, illustrating the wide range of literacy and literary engagement among the Pompeians. The study of graffiti has enriched our understanding of social interactions, public opinion, and individual expression in ancient Rome.

Pompeii's rediscovery and excavation have had a profound impact on the fields of archaeology, art history, and classical studies. The site's extraordinary preservation has provided a wealth of data for researchers, enabling detailed studies of Roman urbanism, architecture, and daily life. The artifacts and artworks from Pompeii have also inspired generations of artists, writers, and scholars, influencing the development of neoclassical art and architecture in the 18th and 19th centuries.

The conservation and management of Pompeii present significant challenges, as the site is exposed to environmental factors such as weathering, erosion, and vegetation growth. Efforts to preserve and protect the site have included stabilization of structures, restoration of frescoes and mosaics, and the implementation of measures to control visitor access and impact. International collaborations and advances in conservation science have played a crucial role in addressing these challenges and ensuring the long-term preservation of Pompeii's invaluable heritage.

In recent years, technological innovations have revolutionized the study and presentation of Pompeii. Techniques such as 3D scanning, digital mapping, and virtual reality have allowed for more accurate documentation and analysis of the site. These technologies have also enhanced public engagement and education, enabling virtual tours and interactive exhibits that bring the ancient city to life for a global audience. The integration of these tools with traditional archaeological methods continues to expand our understanding of Pompeii and its significance.

Chapter 26: Abu Simbel

Abu Simbel is a site of two massive rock temples in southern Egypt, originally carved out of the mountainside during the reign of Pharaoh Ramesses II in the 13th century BCE. Located on the western bank of Lake Nasser, about 230 kilometers southwest of Aswan, these temples are a lasting legacy of the architectural and artistic achievements of ancient Egypt. The complex was initially constructed to demonstrate the power and divine nature of Ramesses II, as well as to commemorate his victory at the Battle of Kadesh and to intimidate his Nubian neighbors. The two temples are often referred to as the Great Temple and the Small Temple, each with its own unique features and significance.

The Great Temple of Abu Simbel, also known as the Temple of Ramesses II, is one of the most awe-inspiring monuments of ancient Egypt. It stands at a height of about 30 meters (98 feet) and extends approximately 35 meters (115 feet) into the mountainside. The facade of the temple is dominated by four colossal statues of Ramesses II, each standing at around 20 meters (66 feet) tall. These statues depict the pharaoh seated on his throne, wearing the double crown of Upper and Lower Egypt, and flanked by smaller statues of his family members, including his mother, Queen Tuya, his wife, Queen Nefertari, and some of his children. The sheer size and grandeur of these statues were intended to convey the might and divine nature of Ramesses II, asserting his dominance and authority.

The entrance to the Great Temple leads to a series of halls and chambers, all adorned with intricate carvings, hieroglyphs, and statues. The first hall, known as the Hypostyle Hall, is supported by eight massive pillars, each carved in the likeness of Ramesses II as Osiris, the god of the afterlife. This hall is decorated with scenes depicting the pharaoh's military campaigns, religious rituals, and interactions with the gods. One of the most notable scenes is the depiction of the Battle of Kadesh, where Ramesses II is shown triumphing over the Hittites, a momentous event in his reign that solidified his reputation as a great warrior king.

Beyond the Hypostyle Hall is the second hall, or the Vestibule, which leads to the inner sanctuary. This sanctuary houses four statues representing the gods Amun-Ra, Ra-Horakhty, Ptah, and a deified Ramesses II. The alignment of the temple is such that twice a year, on February 22 and October 22, the first rays of the morning sun penetrate the temple and illuminate the statues of Amun-Ra, Ra-Horakhty, and Ramesses II, leaving Ptah, the god of the underworld, in shadow. This phenomenon, known as the Solar Illumination, was likely designed to mark significant dates in the pharaoh's life, possibly his coronation and birthday. It is a testament to the advanced understanding of astronomy and engineering possessed by the ancient Egyptians.

The Small Temple, also known as the Temple of Hathor and Nefertari, is located a short distance from the Great Temple. This temple is dedicated to Hathor, the goddess of love and beauty, and to Ramesses II's beloved wife, Queen Nefertari. The facade of the Small Temple features six statues, four of Ramesses II and two of Nefertari, each standing at about 10 meters (33 feet) tall. Unlike other Egyptian temples where the pharaoh's statues are significantly larger than those of his consort, the statues of Nefertari are of equal size to those of Ramesses II, signifying her esteemed status and the pharaoh's deep affection for her.

The interior of the Small Temple is equally impressive, with a Hypostyle Hall supported by six columns adorned with Hathor-headed capitals. The walls are decorated with scenes depicting Nefertari participating in religious rituals, presenting offerings to the gods, and being blessed by Hathor and other deities. These depictions highlight the queen's role in religious and ceremonial life, as well as her close relationship with the divine. The sanctuary of the Small Temple contains a statue of Hathor in the form of a cow, protecting the pharaoh, symbolizing the goddess's nurturing and protective aspects.

The construction of the Abu Simbel temples during the reign of Ramesses II was a monumental engineering feat. The temples were carved directly into the sandstone cliffs, requiring precise planning and skilled labor. The workers, likely numbering in the thousands, included stonemasons, sculptors, painters, and laborers who toiled for around 20 years to complete the project. The temples were originally located on the banks of the Nile River, which played a crucial role in their construction and subsequent history.

Over the centuries, the temples of Abu Simbel were gradually buried under sand and largely forgotten until their rediscovery by Swiss explorer Johann Ludwig Burckhardt in 1813. Subsequent expeditions, including those led by Italian explorer Giovanni Belzoni and French scholar Jean-François Champollion, helped to uncover and document the site. The temples quickly became a focus of scholarly study and attracted visitors from around the world, fascinated by their grandeur and historical significance.

One of the most dramatic episodes in the history of Abu Simbel occurred in the mid-20th century, when the construction of the Aswan High Dam threatened to submerge the temples under the rising waters of Lake Nasser. In response to this threat, an international campaign led by UNESCO was launched to save the temples. Between 1964 and 1968, an extraordinary engineering project was undertaken to relocate the temples to a higher location. The temples were carefully cut into large blocks, each weighing up to 30 tons, and reassembled at a new site 65 meters (213 feet) higher and 200 meters (656 feet) back from the original location. This massive relocation effort, which cost around $40 million, was a landmark achievement in the field of archaeological conservation and highlighted the global importance of preserving cultural heritage.

Today, the temples of Abu Simbel continue to be a major tourist attraction and a symbol of Egypt's rich history and cultural legacy. The site is part of the UNESCO World Heritage Site known as the "Nubian Monuments from Abu Simbel to Philae," which includes other important archaeological sites in the region. Visitors to Abu Simbel can explore the magnificent temples, admire the detailed carvings and paintings, and experience the awe-inspiring Solar Illumination phenomenon.

The significance of Abu Simbel extends beyond its architectural and artistic achievements. The temples are a testament to the political, religious, and cultural dynamics of ancient Egypt during the New Kingdom period. They reflect the power and ambition of Ramesses II, one of Egypt's most celebrated pharaohs, who sought to immortalize his legacy through monumental construction projects. The temples also provide valuable insights into the religious practices and beliefs of the ancient Egyptians, illustrating their reverence for the gods and the pharaoh's role as a divine intermediary.

The art and iconography of Abu Simbel are rich in symbolism and meaning. The colossal statues of Ramesses II, with their imposing size and serene expressions, convey the pharaoh's divine status and authority. The scenes of military triumph, religious ceremonies, and offerings to the gods emphasize the pharaoh's role as a warrior, priest, and protector of the land. The depictions of Nefertari and her close association with Hathor highlight the queen's significance and the integration of royal women into the religious and ceremonial life of ancient Egypt.

In addition to their historical and cultural value, the temples of Abu Simbel have inspired countless artistic and literary works. The grandeur and mystery of the site have captivated the imaginations of writers, poets, and artists, who have sought to capture its essence in their creations. The story of Abu Simbel, from its construction and rediscovery to its dramatic rescue and relocation, continues to resonate

with people around the world, symbolizing the enduring human quest
to preserve and celebrate our shared heritage.

Chapter 27: The Ziggurat of Ur

The Ziggurat of Ur, one of the most significant and impressive architectural feats of the ancient world, stands as a testament to the ingenuity, religious devotion, and engineering prowess of the Sumerian civilization. Located in present-day Iraq near Nasiriyah, this massive structure was built during the early Bronze Age, around the 21st century BCE, by King Ur-Nammu of the Third Dynasty of Ur. Dedicated to Nanna, the moon god, the ziggurat served as the focal point of religious life in the city of Ur and exemplified the ziggurat architectural form that characterized the religious complexes of ancient Mesopotamia.

The Ziggurat of Ur was originally constructed as a terraced pyramid with a rectangular base measuring approximately 64 by 45 meters and rising to an estimated height of about 30 meters. Its core was made of mud bricks, which were then covered with baked bricks set in bitumen, a naturally occurring tar-like substance used as mortar. This construction technique not only provided structural stability but also offered some protection against the harsh climatic conditions of the region. The ziggurat's design featured three distinct levels, each slightly smaller than the one below it, creating a stepped appearance. A broad, central staircase, flanked by two smaller staircases, led to the summit, where a temple or shrine was believed to be located.

The purpose of the ziggurat was deeply rooted in the religious beliefs of the Sumerians. As a man-made mountain, it symbolized the connection between the heavens and the earth, serving as a bridge between the human and divine realms. The elevated temple at the top of the ziggurat was thought to be the dwelling place of Nanna, where priests would conduct rituals, offer sacrifices, and communicate with the deity on behalf of the people. This sacred space was not accessible to the general populace, emphasizing the role of the priesthood as intermediaries between the gods and humans.

The construction of the Ziggurat of Ur under King Ur-Nammu marked a period of significant cultural and political development in Mesopotamia. Ur-Nammu's reign is notable for the establishment of the first recorded legal code, the Code of Ur-Nammu, which predated the more famous Code of Hammurabi by several centuries. His ambitious building projects, including the ziggurat, aimed to reinforce his authority, demonstrate his piety, and promote the prosperity of his kingdom. The construction of such monumental architecture required the mobilization of vast resources and labor, reflecting the organizational capabilities of the Sumerian state.

The ziggurat was not only a religious center but also a symbol of the city of Ur's wealth, power, and technological advancement. Ur, located near the confluence of the Tigris and Euphrates rivers, was a major hub of trade, culture, and administration in ancient Mesopotamia. Its strategic location facilitated commerce and communication with other regions, contributing to the city's prosperity. The ziggurat, towering over the city, would have been visible from a great distance, serving as a constant reminder of the divine favor and royal authority that underpinned Ur's prominence.

Over the centuries, the Ziggurat of Ur underwent several phases of restoration and reconstruction, reflecting its enduring significance in Mesopotamian culture. After the decline of the Third Dynasty of Ur, the ziggurat continued to be revered and maintained by subsequent rulers, including the Kassites and Neo-Babylonians. Notably, King Nabonidus of Babylon, who reigned in the 6th century BCE, undertook extensive restoration work on the ziggurat, recognizing its historical and religious importance. These efforts ensured that the ziggurat remained a vital part of the cultural and spiritual landscape of Mesopotamia for many generations.

The rediscovery and excavation of the Ziggurat of Ur in the 19th and 20th centuries have provided invaluable insights into the history and culture of ancient Mesopotamia. Initial explorations by European travelers and scholars, such as William Loftus in the mid-19th century, were followed by more systematic excavations led by Sir Leonard Woolley in the 1920s and 1930s. Woolley's work at Ur uncovered not only the ziggurat but also the Royal Cemetery of Ur, which yielded a wealth of artifacts, including the famous Standard of Ur and the gold and lapis lazuli treasures of Queen Puabi. These discoveries have significantly enriched our understanding of Sumerian civilization, its social structure, and its artistic achievements.

The Ziggurat of Ur has also played a crucial role in the study of Mesopotamian architecture and urban planning. Its design, with its stepped terraces and central staircase, set a precedent for later ziggurats built throughout the region. These structures served as prototypes for subsequent monumental architecture in Mesopotamia and influenced the development of religious complexes in neighboring cultures. The ziggurat's construction techniques, including the use of mud brick and bitumen, illustrate the technological innovations and adaptive strategies employed by the Sumerians to build enduring structures in their challenging environment.

The ziggurat's symbolic significance extends beyond its architectural and religious functions. It embodies the Sumerians' cosmological worldview, which envisioned the world as a series of concentric layers, with the earth at the center and the heavens above. The ziggurat, as a man-made mountain, represented an axis mundi, or world axis, connecting these layers and facilitating communication between humans and the divine. This concept of sacred architecture as a microcosm of the universe has parallels in other ancient cultures, reflecting a common human desire to create tangible links to the divine.

In addition to its religious and symbolic importance, the Ziggurat of Ur played a central role in the social and economic life of the city. The temple complex associated with the ziggurat was a major center of economic activity, serving as a repository for agricultural surplus, a hub for trade, and a center for craft production. The temple administration managed vast estates, collected taxes, and employed a large workforce, including priests, scribes, craftsmen, and laborers. This economic function underscored the integration of religious, political, and economic power in Sumerian society, with the temple acting as both a spiritual and administrative center.

The Ziggurat of Ur also reflects the artistic achievements of the Sumerians. The detailed brickwork, the symmetry of the structure, and the decorative elements, such as the use of glazed bricks and intricate mosaics, highlight the aesthetic sensibilities and craftsmanship of the builders. The ziggurat's design, with its imposing scale and harmonious proportions, demonstrates a sophisticated understanding of architectural principles and an ability to create monumental structures that convey a sense of awe and reverence.

In modern times, the Ziggurat of Ur continues to capture the imagination of scholars, historians, and the general public. Its preservation and study offer a window into the early history of urban civilization and the development of complex societies in Mesopotamia. The site has been a focal point for archaeological research, heritage conservation, and cultural tourism, contributing to the broader appreciation of ancient Mesopotamian culture and its enduring legacy.

The political and social turmoil in Iraq over the past decades has posed significant challenges to the preservation and protection of the Ziggurat of Ur. Efforts by local and international organizations to safeguard the site and promote its conservation have been crucial in ensuring that this invaluable heritage is not lost to conflict and neglect. The ziggurat stands as a symbol of the rich cultural heritage of Iraq and the broader Middle East, highlighting the need for continued efforts to preserve and celebrate the achievements of ancient civilizations.

Chapter 28: The Pyramids of Meroë

The Pyramids of Meroë, located in present-day Sudan, are one of the most fascinating and lesser-known marvels of the ancient world. These pyramids, constructed by the Kingdom of Kush, provide a profound glimpse into the civilization that thrived south of ancient Egypt. The Kingdom of Kush, with its capital at Meroë, flourished for several centuries, from around 800 BCE to 350 CE, and was notable for its unique blend of indigenous African and Egyptian influences. The pyramids at Meroë, which served as royal tombs, are a testament to the sophisticated cultural and architectural achievements of this civilization.

Meroë, situated on the east bank of the Nile River, became the primary royal cemetery of the Kushite kingdom. The site comprises three major necropolises: the South Cemetery, the North Cemetery, and the West Cemetery, with over 200 pyramids in total. These pyramids differ significantly from their Egyptian counterparts in both design and construction. While Egyptian pyramids are known for their massive size and smooth, limestone exteriors, the Kushite pyramids are much smaller and steeper, often featuring a stepped appearance. Despite their smaller size, they are no less impressive, reflecting a high degree of architectural skill and cultural significance.

The pyramids of Meroë were built as the final resting places for the kings, queens, and nobles of Kush. Each pyramid typically sat atop a tomb chamber that was cut into the bedrock beneath it. These tomb chambers were often elaborately decorated with murals depicting scenes of the deceased's life, as well as religious and mythological motifs. The pyramids themselves were constructed using local sandstone, and many were adorned with intricate carvings and hieroglyphic inscriptions that detailed the achievements and titles of the buried individuals.

One of the distinguishing features of the Meroitic pyramids is their funerary chapels, which were built adjacent to the pyramids. These chapels served as places for offerings and rituals to honor the deceased and ensure their safe passage to the afterlife. The chapels were decorated with reliefs and paintings that depicted the journey of the soul, rituals performed by priests, and scenes of the afterlife. This practice reflects the Kushite belief in the afterlife and their reverence for the deceased, similar to the beliefs held by the ancient Egyptians.

The pyramids at Meroë represent a fusion of Egyptian and indigenous African elements. The Kushites adopted many aspects of Egyptian culture, including the practice of pyramid building, as a result of their prolonged interactions with Egypt. During the 25th Dynasty, also known as the Nubian Dynasty, the Kushite kings even ruled over Egypt for nearly a century, further intensifying the cultural exchange between the two regions. However, the Kushites adapted and modified these influences to create a distinct architectural style that was uniquely their own.

The construction of the pyramids at Meroë marked a significant period in the history of the Kingdom of Kush, particularly during the Meroitic Period (c. 300 BCE to 350 CE). This era saw the kingdom reach its zenith in terms of political power, economic prosperity, and cultural achievements. Meroë became a major center of trade, connecting sub-Saharan Africa with the Mediterranean world. The city was renowned for its iron production, a key industry that contributed to the kingdom's wealth and influence. The iron tools and weapons produced in Meroë were highly sought after and played a crucial role in the kingdom's military and economic strength.

The wealth generated by trade and industry allowed the rulers of Meroë to commission grand architectural projects, including the construction of the pyramids. These structures not only served as tombs but also as symbols of royal power and divine authority. The pyramids were strategically located to be visible from a distance, reinforcing the presence and prestige of the Kushite kings and queens. The prominence of female rulers, or kandakes, in Kushite society is another notable aspect, with several queens buried in the pyramids at Meroë, highlighting the significant role women played in the political and religious life of the kingdom.

The religious practices of the Kushites, as reflected in the pyramids of Meroë, were deeply influenced by Egyptian traditions, yet they also incorporated indigenous elements. The worship of gods such as Amun, Isis, and Osiris was central to their belief system, but the Kushites also venerated local deities, including Apedemak, the lion-headed god of war. The iconography and symbolism found in the tombs and chapels often depicted these deities, illustrating the syncretic nature of Kushite religion. The pyramids thus served as important religious monuments, linking the Kushite rulers to the divine and legitimizing their authority.

The decline of the Kingdom of Kush and the abandonment of Meroë around the mid-4th century CE remain subjects of scholarly debate. Various factors, including economic decline, environmental changes, and external pressures from neighboring civilizations, likely contributed to the downfall of this once-great kingdom. Despite the decline, the pyramids of Meroë endured as silent witnesses to the grandeur of the Kushite civilization. Over the centuries, the site was largely forgotten by the outside world until its rediscovery in the 19th century by European explorers.

The rediscovery of the pyramids of Meroë sparked significant interest among archaeologists and historians, leading to numerous expeditions and excavations. The pioneering work of scholars such as Giuseppe Ferlini in the 1830s, who infamously destroyed some of the pyramids in search of treasure, and later more scientific explorations by the likes of Karl Richard Lepsius and George Andrew Reisner, helped to bring the history and significance of the Kushite civilization to light. These explorations uncovered a wealth of artifacts, including jewelry, pottery, and tools, which have provided invaluable insights into the daily life, culture, and artistry of the Kushites.

In modern times, the pyramids of Meroë have gained recognition as a UNESCO World Heritage site, emphasizing their global cultural and historical significance. Efforts to preserve and protect these ancient structures have been undertaken by both local and international organizations. The site attracts scholars, historians, and tourists, all eager to explore and understand the legacy of the Kingdom of Kush. The preservation of the pyramids is crucial not only for Sudanese heritage but also for the broader understanding of ancient African civilizations and their contributions to human history.

The architectural and cultural heritage of the pyramids of Meroë continues to inspire contemporary scholars and enthusiasts. Their unique style and historical context challenge the traditionally Egypt-centric view of ancient African history, highlighting the independent and influential nature of the Kushite civilization. The study of these pyramids offers a more nuanced understanding of the interactions between ancient cultures and the diverse expressions of architectural and religious practices across different regions.

The Pyramids of Meroë, with their distinctive design and rich historical context, stand as a testament to the enduring legacy of the Kingdom of Kush. They represent a civilization that thrived through its ingenuity, trade, and cultural synthesis, creating monuments that continue to fascinate and inform. The story of Meroë and its pyramids is a vital chapter in the broader narrative of human civilization, illustrating the complexities and achievements of ancient African societies. As research and conservation efforts continue, the pyramids of Meroë will undoubtedly remain a source of inspiration and knowledge for generations to come.

Chapter 29: Hampi

Hampi, located in the southern Indian state of Karnataka, is an ancient village that once served as the prosperous capital of the Vijayanagara Empire. The site is renowned for its extensive ruins, which cover a sprawling area of more than 4,100 hectares, making it one of the largest archaeological sites in India. Hampi's significance is not only historical but also architectural and cultural, earning it a place as a UNESCO World Heritage Site in 1986.

The history of Hampi dates back to the 1st century AD, but its most glorious period began in the mid-14th century when it became the capital of the Vijayanagara Empire. The empire was established by Harihara I and his brother Bukka Raya I, and it soon grew into one of the most powerful and prosperous kingdoms in South India. The strategic location of Hampi, on the banks of the Tungabhadra River and surrounded by rugged granite hills, made it a natural fortress, difficult to besiege and easy to defend.

Hampi's landscape is dotted with a multitude of temples, palaces, markets, and other structures that reflect the grandeur of the Vijayanagara Empire. Among the most prominent landmarks is the Virupaksha Temple, dedicated to Lord Shiva. This temple has been a significant center of pilgrimage for centuries and continues to be an active place of worship. The temple complex includes a massive towered gateway, intricately carved pillars, and a sanctum sanctorum that houses the deity. The Virupaksha Temple is also notable for its annual chariot festival, which attracts thousands of devotees.

Another iconic structure in Hampi is the Vittala Temple, renowned for its extraordinary architecture and unmatched craftsmanship. The temple complex is famous for its musical pillars, which produce musical notes when struck, and the iconic stone chariot that stands in front of the temple. The chariot, a stunning piece of artistry, symbolizes the pinnacle of Vijayanagara architecture. The

Vittala Temple complex also features a large courtyard and numerous halls, each adorned with elaborate carvings depicting various deities, mythological scenes, and daily life in the empire.

The Royal Enclosure is another significant area in Hampi, which served as the administrative and ceremonial center of the Vijayanagara Empire. This expansive complex includes several important structures, such as the Mahanavami Dibba, an enormous platform where the king once viewed the Dasara festival celebrations, and the King's Audience Hall, where the ruler addressed his subjects and held court. The Royal Enclosure also contains the Queen's Bath, an ornate structure with a sunken bath surrounded by a gallery and decorative arches, showcasing the luxurious lifestyle of the royal family.

Hampi is also home to the Lotus Mahal, a unique structure within the Zenana Enclosure, an area reserved for the royal women. The Lotus Mahal combines Hindu and Islamic architectural styles, evident in its arched windows and domed towers. The structure is named for its lotus-like appearance and is believed to have been used as a recreational pavilion by the royal ladies.

The Hampi Bazaar, located near the Virupaksha Temple, was once a bustling marketplace that attracted traders from all over the world. This long street was lined with shops selling precious stones, spices, textiles, and other goods, reflecting the cosmopolitan nature of the Vijayanagara Empire. Today, the remnants of the bazaar provide a glimpse into the vibrant trade and commerce that flourished in Hampi during its heyday.

The Sasivekalu Ganesha and the Kadalekalu Ganesha are two monolithic statues of Lord Ganesha located in Hampi. These massive sculptures, carved out of single boulders, exemplify the artistic prowess of the Vijayanagara sculptors. The Sasivekalu Ganesha, named for its resemblance to a mustard seed, stands at around 2.4 meters tall, while the Kadalekalu Ganesha, resembling a Bengal gram, is even larger, measuring about 4.5 meters in height.

Hampi's architectural marvels extend beyond religious and royal edifices. The site is dotted with numerous step wells, such as the Pushkarini, which were used for religious rituals and as water sources. These step wells are intricately designed with symmetrical steps and ornate carvings, highlighting the advanced engineering and aesthetic sensibilities of the Vijayanagara period.

One cannot discuss Hampi without mentioning the Matanga Hill, which offers a panoramic view of the entire site. The hill is associated with the Ramayana, as it is believed to be the place where Lord Hanuman met Lord Rama and informed him about Sita's whereabouts. The summit of Matanga Hill is marked by a small temple, and the trek to the top is a popular activity for visitors seeking to witness the breathtaking sunrise or sunset over the ancient ruins.

Hampi's significance extends beyond its architectural grandeur; it is also a repository of the rich cultural heritage of the Vijayanagara Empire. The empire was known for its patronage of art, literature, and music, and Hampi served as a vibrant cultural hub. Renowned poets, scholars, and artists thrived under the patronage of the Vijayanagara kings, contributing to a flourishing cultural landscape that left an indelible mark on South Indian history.

The decline of Hampi began in 1565 after the catastrophic Battle of Talikota, where the combined forces of the Deccan Sultanates defeated the Vijayanagara army. The city was ransacked, and its magnificent structures were left in ruins. Despite this, the remnants of Hampi continue to stand as a testament to the grandeur and sophistication of the Vijayanagara Empire.

The rediscovery of Hampi by European explorers in the 19th century brought the site to international attention, sparking interest among historians, archaeologists, and travelers. Today, Hampi is a major tourist destination, attracting visitors from around the world who come to marvel at its ancient ruins and immerse themselves in its historical legacy. Efforts to preserve and restore Hampi's monuments are ongoing, ensuring that future generations can continue to appreciate and learn from this remarkable window into India's past.

Chapter 30: Mycenae

Mycenae, an ancient city in Greece, holds a prominent place in the annals of classical history and mythology. Situated in the northeastern Peloponnese, Mycenae was one of the major centers of Greek civilization during the second millennium BCE, approximately from 1600 to 1100 BCE, and is considered a pivotal site in the study of Mycenaean culture. The city's enduring fame is partly due to its association with Homer's epics, "The Iliad" and "The Odyssey," where it is depicted as the seat of King Agamemnon, the leader of the Greeks during the Trojan War.

The archaeological site of Mycenae, first excavated by Heinrich Schliemann in the late 19th century, reveals a wealth of historical and cultural treasures. The city is strategically located on a hill overlooking the fertile Argolid plain, with a commanding view of the surrounding region, which helped it to become a powerful and influential city-state. The location provided natural defenses, with the city encircled by steep hills and the only accessible approach being through a narrow gorge, making it an ideal site for a fortified settlement.

One of the most striking features of Mycenae is the Lion Gate, the main entrance to the citadel. The gate, constructed around 1250 BCE, is an imposing structure made of massive limestone blocks. It is named after the relief sculpture of two lions, or possibly lionesses, that stands above the entrance. The Lion Gate is an iconic symbol of Mycenaean architecture and showcases the civilization's advanced engineering skills and artistic sensibilities. The gate leads into the fortified acropolis, which was the heart of Mycenaean political and religious life.

Within the acropolis, the palace complex of Mycenae is a focal point. The palace, built on multiple terraces, was the residence of the ruling elite and served as the administrative and ceremonial center of the city. The complex includes a central megaron, a large hall with a throne room and a central hearth, surrounded by smaller rooms used for various functions, including storage, workshops, and living quarters. The megaron is particularly significant as it reflects the architectural style that would later influence the design of Greek temples.

Mycenae is also renowned for its elaborate tombs, which provide valuable insights into the burial practices and beliefs of the Mycenaeans. The most famous of these is the Treasury of Atreus, also known as the Tomb of Agamemnon. This tholos, or beehive-shaped tomb, is one of the largest and most impressive examples of Mycenaean funerary architecture. Constructed around 1250 BCE, the Treasury of Atreus features a long dromos, or entrance passage, leading to a massive doorway adorned with decorative stonework. The interior of the tomb is a circular chamber with a corbelled dome, created by layering stones in a precise and sophisticated manner to form a self-supporting structure. The tomb's grandeur and scale underscore the wealth and power of the Mycenaean elite.

Another significant burial site is Grave Circle A, located within the citadel walls. This royal cemetery, dating to the 16th century BCE, contains six shaft graves that were used for multiple burials. Excavations of these graves uncovered a wealth of grave goods, including gold masks, jewelry, weapons, and other artifacts, indicating the high status of the individuals buried there. The most famous find from Grave Circle A is the so-called Mask of Agamemnon, a gold funeral mask discovered by Schliemann, which he believed to be the death mask of the legendary king. Although the identification is now considered unlikely, the mask remains an iconic artifact of Mycenaean art.

Outside the acropolis, the city of Mycenae extended into the surrounding plains, where additional residential areas, workshops, and burial sites have been discovered. These areas provide further evidence of the complexity and sophistication of Mycenaean society. The extensive fortifications, advanced engineering, and wealth of the city reflect a highly organized and hierarchical society, with a powerful ruling class that controlled vast resources and exerted influence over a wide area.

Mycenaean culture is characterized by its distinctive art and architecture, as well as its contributions to the development of Greek civilization. The Mycenaeans were skilled artisans, producing intricate pottery, frescoes, metalwork, and jewelry. Their pottery, often decorated with geometric patterns and scenes of warfare and hunting, is notable for its technical precision and artistic quality. Frescoes from Mycenaean sites depict scenes of daily life, religious rituals, and mythological themes, providing valuable insights into the culture and beliefs of the Mycenaeans.

The Mycenaeans were also accomplished builders, as evidenced by their monumental architecture and sophisticated engineering techniques. They constructed large palatial complexes, fortified citadels, and extensive hydraulic systems for water management. Their use of massive stone blocks in construction, known as Cyclopean masonry, is a hallmark of Mycenaean architecture and reflects their ability to organize and mobilize large labor forces.

The decline of Mycenae, like that of other Mycenaean centers, occurred around 1100 BCE, marking the end of the Late Bronze Age in Greece. The reasons for this decline are still debated among scholars, with theories ranging from natural disasters and climate change to internal strife and invasions by external groups, such as the Sea Peoples. Whatever the cause, the fall of Mycenae led to a period of economic and cultural decline known as the Greek Dark Ages.

Despite its decline, the legacy of Mycenae continued to influence Greek culture for centuries. The Mycenaean civilization laid the foundations for many aspects of later Greek culture, including language, art, architecture, and religious practices. The myths and legends associated with Mycenae, particularly those recorded in

Homeric epics, became an integral part of Greek cultural identity and continued to be celebrated in literature and art.

In modern times, the archaeological site of Mycenae attracts scholars and tourists alike, eager to explore its ancient ruins and uncover the secrets of its past. Ongoing excavations and research continue to shed light on the complexities of Mycenaean society and its contributions to the broader history of the ancient world. The site's inclusion in the UNESCO World Heritage list in 1999 underscores its global significance and the need for its preservation.

Chapter 31: Persepolis

Persepolis, known as Takht-e Jamshid in modern Iran, is one of the most significant archaeological sites of the ancient world, embodying the grandeur and sophistication of the Achaemenid Empire. Located in the Fars Province of Iran, Persepolis was the ceremonial capital of the Achaemenid Empire, which spanned from the 6th to the 4th century BCE. Founded by Darius I in 518 BCE, Persepolis served as the heart of the empire, where rulers conducted official ceremonies and received tribute from across the vast territories they controlled. The city stands as a testament to the empire's architectural and artistic achievements, reflecting the power, diversity, and cultural integration of the Achaemenid dynasty.

The construction of Persepolis was an ambitious project initiated by Darius I and continued by his successors, including Xerxes I and Artaxerxes I. The site was carefully chosen in a remote mountainous region, providing natural defenses and a strategic location. The main terrace, which covers an area of approximately 125,000 square meters, was built on an artificially leveled platform with a series of terraces ascending from the plain below. This grand terrace was the foundation for the city's most important buildings and structures, showcasing the Achaemenids' advanced engineering skills and their ability to mobilize resources and labor on an immense scale.

One of the most iconic features of Persepolis is the Apadana, or the Audience Hall, constructed by Darius I and completed by Xerxes I. This massive hall, measuring 60 meters on each side and supported by 72 columns, was used for official audiences and receptions. The columns, standing over 20 meters tall, were topped with elaborate capitals featuring double-headed bulls, lions, and other mythical creatures. The Apadana's walls were adorned with intricate bas-reliefs depicting scenes of tribute-bearing delegations from various subject nations of the empire, highlighting the Achaemenids' ability to govern a vast and culturally diverse empire. These reliefs are a remarkable example of Achaemenid art, characterized by their detailed and realistic portrayal of people, animals, and ceremonial processions.

Another significant structure at Persepolis is the Tachara, or the palace of Darius I. This smaller yet equally impressive building was used as a private residence and reception hall by the king. The Tachara's walls are covered with finely carved reliefs depicting royal scenes, courtiers, and attendants. One of the notable features of the Tachara is the "Gate of All Nations," a grand entrance hall with two colossal winged bulls flanking the gateway. This gate symbolized the empire's inclusiveness, welcoming representatives from all the nations under Achaemenid rule.

The Hadish, the palace of Xerxes I, is another important structure within the Persepolis complex. This palace, located on the southern part of the terrace, was the largest and most opulent of all the royal residences at Persepolis. The Hadish featured a central hall with 36 columns, surrounded by smaller rooms and chambers, each decorated with intricate reliefs and carvings. The palace's location and its architectural grandeur reflect Xerxes I's ambition to surpass his predecessors in both power and prestige.

The Hall of a Hundred Columns, also known as the Throne Hall, is another monumental building at Persepolis. This hall, completed by Artaxerxes I, was used for official ceremonies and royal receptions. The hall's name derives from the 100 columns that supported its roof, each standing over 12 meters tall. The interior walls of the Throne Hall were decorated with reliefs depicting the king enthroned, surrounded by his attendants and bodyguards, emphasizing the central role of the monarch in the Achaemenid political and religious hierarchy.

Persepolis also housed several significant treasury buildings, which stored the vast wealth accumulated by the Achaemenid rulers. These buildings, located in the northeastern part of the terrace, were heavily fortified and guarded, reflecting the immense value of their contents. The treasury buildings contained not only gold and silver but also precious artifacts, luxury goods, and tribute from across the empire. The discovery of these treasures during excavations has provided valuable insights into the economic and cultural richness of the Achaemenid Empire.

The extensive use of stone in the construction of Persepolis, particularly limestone and other local materials, is a testament to the Achaemenid's advanced architectural techniques. The city's builders employed a sophisticated method of stone carving and fitting, with blocks cut precisely to interlock without the use of mortar. This technique not only ensured the structural stability of the buildings but also allowed for the creation of intricate carvings and reliefs that have withstood the test of time.

One of the most striking aspects of Persepolis is its integration of various artistic and architectural styles from across the Achaemenid Empire. The city's builders and artists drew inspiration from the diverse cultures and traditions within the empire, including Mesopotamian, Egyptian, Anatolian, and Greek influences. This cultural synthesis is evident in the design of the buildings, the motifs used in the reliefs, and the overall aesthetic of the city. The result is a unique and harmonious blend of artistic traditions that reflect the cosmopolitan nature of the Achaemenid Empire.

The ceremonial nature of Persepolis is further highlighted by the numerous inscriptions and texts found at the site. These inscriptions, written in Old Persian, Elamite, and Babylonian, provide valuable information about the construction of the city, the genealogy of the Achaemenid kings, and the administrative organization of the empire. One of the most important inscriptions is the Darius inscription, which details the construction of the Apadana and other buildings at Persepolis and emphasizes the king's role as a pious and just ruler.

The destruction of Persepolis is a significant event in the history of the ancient world. In 330 BCE, the city was sacked and burned by Alexander the Great during his campaign to conquer the Achaemenid

Empire. The reasons for this destruction are debated among historians, with some suggesting it was a deliberate act of retribution for the Persian invasion of Greece and the burning of Athens, while others believe it was an impulsive act fueled by a drunken revelry. Regardless of the motivations, the destruction of Persepolis marked the end of the Achaemenid dynasty and the beginning of a new era under Alexander and his successors.

Despite its destruction, the ruins of Persepolis have continued to captivate scholars and visitors for centuries. The site was largely forgotten until the 17th century when European travelers began to explore the region and document their findings. Systematic excavations of Persepolis began in the early 20th century, led by archaeologists such as Ernst Herzfeld and Erich Schmidt. These excavations uncovered a wealth of artifacts, inscriptions, and architectural elements that have provided invaluable insights into the history, culture, and achievements of the Achaemenid Empire.

Today, Persepolis is recognized as a UNESCO World Heritage Site and is one of Iran's most important cultural and historical landmarks. The site attracts thousands of tourists each year, who come to marvel at its architectural splendor and to gain a deeper understanding of the Achaemenid civilization. Efforts to preserve and protect Persepolis continue, with ongoing conservation projects aimed at maintaining the integrity of the site and ensuring that it can be enjoyed by future generations.

Chapter 32: Mohenjo-Daro

Mohenjo-Daro, one of the most remarkable urban centers of the ancient world, stands as a testament to the ingenuity, sophistication, and organization of the Indus Valley Civilization. Located in present-day Sindh, Pakistan, Mohenjo-Daro, which means "Mound of the Dead," is believed to have been built around 2500 BCE and was one of the largest settlements of the ancient Indus Valley Civilization. Its discovery in the 1920s by British archaeologist Sir John Marshall marked a pivotal moment in understanding early urbanization in South Asia and revealed the advanced nature of this ancient society.

The city of Mohenjo-Daro was meticulously planned and constructed, displaying a high level of urban planning and civil engineering. It covered approximately 300 hectares, with its layout based on a grid pattern. This grid system, featuring straight streets intersecting at right angles, indicates an advanced understanding of urban planning principles. The city was divided into two main parts: the Citadel and the Lower City. The Citadel, located on a raised mound, housed large public buildings, granaries, and possibly administrative and religious structures, while the Lower City contained residential areas, markets, and workshops.

One of the most striking features of Mohenjo-Daro is its sophisticated drainage and sanitation system. The city's planners constructed an intricate network of brick-lined drains that ran along the streets, connected to individual houses and public baths. These drains, covered with bricks or stone slabs, efficiently removed wastewater and rainwater, demonstrating an advanced understanding of public health and hygiene. Many houses were equipped with private wells, bathrooms, and toilets, which were connected to the main drainage system, underscoring the emphasis on cleanliness and sanitation in this ancient society.

The Great Bath, located in the Citadel area, is one of the most iconic structures of Mohenjo-Daro. Measuring approximately 12 meters by 7 meters, with a depth of 2.4 meters, the Great Bath was constructed with finely fitted bricks and was waterproofed with bitumen. It is believed to have been used for ritual bathing or religious ceremonies, highlighting the importance of water in the cultural and religious practices of the Indus Valley Civilization. The presence of this elaborate bathing facility suggests a high degree of social organization and the existence of communal activities.

Residential buildings in Mohenjo-Daro were constructed using baked bricks, a testament to the technological advancement of the Indus Valley people. The houses varied in size, indicating a possible social hierarchy, but most were designed with similar features, including central courtyards, multiple rooms, and staircases leading to upper floors or rooftops. The presence of standardized brick sizes and uniform construction techniques across the city points to a highly organized and regulated construction industry. Many houses also had access to water through private wells, and some even had bathrooms and toilets connected to the city's drainage system.

Artifacts recovered from Mohenjo-Daro provide valuable insights into the daily life, culture, and economy of its inhabitants. Pottery, tools, jewelry, and toys have been found in abundance, indicating a thriving and diverse material culture. The discovery of seals, often made of steatite and engraved with animal motifs and undeciphered script, suggests a system of trade and administration. These seals, which were likely used for commercial and administrative purposes, provide evidence of a complex economic system that included trade with distant regions, including Mesopotamia.

The Indus script, found on numerous seals and pottery fragments, remains one of the most enigmatic aspects of the Indus Valley Civilization. Despite numerous attempts, this script has not been deciphered, leaving many aspects of the society, including their language, political system, and religious beliefs, shrouded in mystery. The script's undeciphered nature has limited our understanding of the intellectual and administrative capabilities of the people of Mohenjo-Daro, but its widespread use indicates a high degree of literacy and record-keeping.

Agriculture was the backbone of Mohenjo-Daro's economy. The fertile plains of the Indus River provided ideal conditions for farming, and the inhabitants cultivated a variety of crops, including wheat, barley, and peas. Evidence of sophisticated irrigation systems, such as canals and reservoirs, suggests that the people of Mohenjo-Daro practiced advanced agricultural techniques to manage water resources and support large-scale farming. This agricultural surplus likely supported a dense population and facilitated trade with neighboring regions.

Trade and commerce played a significant role in the prosperity of Mohenjo-Daro. The city's strategic location along the Indus River facilitated trade with other parts of the Indus Valley and distant regions. Artifacts such as beads, pottery, and seals have been found in Mesopotamia, indicating that Mohenjo-Daro was part of a vast trade network that extended to the Persian Gulf and beyond. This exchange of goods and ideas would have contributed to the cultural and economic dynamism of the city.

The social structure of Mohenjo-Daro, while not fully understood, appears to have been complex and hierarchical. The size and layout of residential buildings suggest a stratified society with varying degrees of wealth and status. Public buildings and granaries indicate a centralized authority responsible for the storage and distribution of surplus agricultural produce, suggesting an organized and possibly bureaucratic administration. The absence of monumental structures dedicated to rulers, such as palaces or large statues, contrasts with contemporary civilizations like Egypt and Mesopotamia and raises questions about the nature of political and religious leadership in the Indus Valley Civilization.

The religious beliefs and practices of the people of Mohenjo-Daro remain largely speculative due to the lack of decipherable written records. However, archaeological evidence provides some clues. The Great Bath suggests the importance of water in ritualistic activities, possibly indicating a form of water worship or purification rites. Numerous terracotta figurines, often depicting female figures, suggest the worship of mother goddesses or fertility deities. Additionally, the presence of various animal motifs on seals and pottery indicates that animals played a significant role in the religious and cultural symbolism of the Indus Valley people.

The decline and eventual abandonment of Mohenjo-Daro around 1900 BCE remains a subject of debate among scholars. Various theories have been proposed, including climate change, river course shifts, overuse of natural resources, and invasions by external groups such as the Aryans. Some evidence suggests that environmental changes, such as the drying up of the Ghaggar-Hakra River system, may have disrupted agricultural production and led to the decline of the city. The exact cause of the city's decline, however, remains uncertain and continues to be a topic of ongoing research and exploration.

Today, Mohenjo-Daro stands as a UNESCO World Heritage Site and a symbol of Pakistan's rich cultural heritage. Ongoing archaeological research and conservation efforts aim to preserve this invaluable site for future generations. The ruins of Mohenjo-Daro continue to inspire awe and curiosity, offering a glimpse into a sophisticated and enigmatic civilization that flourished over four millennia ago. As archaeologists and scholars continue to uncover its secrets, Mohenjo-Daro promises to shed further light on the early urbanization, cultural practices, and technological advancements of the Indus Valley Civilization.

Chapter 33: The Forum Romanum

The Forum Romanum, or Roman Forum, is one of the most iconic and historically significant archaeological sites in the world. Situated in the heart of ancient Rome, it served as the political, commercial, and social hub of the Roman Empire for over a thousand years. The Forum was the epicenter of Roman public life, where citizens gathered to conduct business, discuss politics, worship the gods, and celebrate military triumphs. It evolved from a simple marketplace into a sprawling complex of temples, basilicas, and public spaces, reflecting the growth and grandeur of Rome from its early Republic days to the height of the Empire.

The origins of the Forum Romanum date back to the 7th century BCE, during the early days of Rome's monarchy. Initially, it was a marshy valley situated between the Palatine and Capitoline hills, but it was drained by the construction of the Cloaca Maxima, one of the world's earliest sewage systems. This allowed the area to be developed into a public space. The Forum's early structures were modest, primarily wooden buildings serving as markets and meeting places.

As Rome transitioned from a monarchy to a republic in the late 6th century BCE, the Forum began to take on a more formalized role in public life. The construction of the Regia, the official residence of the kings and later the office of the Pontifex Maximus (chief priest), marked the beginning of the Forum's transformation. The Comitium, an open-air public meeting space, was also established during this period, serving as the focal point for political activities and assemblies.

The Republican era saw significant development in the Forum Romanum. Around 500 BCE, the Senate House, or Curia, was constructed, providing a dedicated space for the Roman Senate to convene. This building underwent several reconstructions over the centuries, with the most famous being the Curia Julia, built by Julius Caesar. The Forum's importance as a political center was further solidified by the erection of the Rostra, a large platform for public speeches. The Rostra was adorned with the prows of captured ships, symbolizing Roman naval victories.

The Forum's religious significance grew with the construction of several temples dedicated to various deities. One of the earliest and most important was the Temple of Vesta, dedicated to the goddess of the hearth. The Vestal Virgins, priestesses who tended the sacred fire of Vesta, resided in the nearby House of the Vestals. Other significant temples included the Temple of Saturn, housing the state treasury, and the Temple of Castor and Pollux, commemorating the legendary twin brothers who were believed to have aided the Romans in battle.

The late Republic period witnessed further expansion and beautification of the Forum. Julius Caesar initiated several building projects, including the construction of the Basilica Julia, a large public building used for legal proceedings and other civic functions. Caesar also began the Forum of Caesar, a new forum adjacent to the Forum Romanum, which included the Temple of Venus Genetrix, honoring his divine ancestor.

The transition from Republic to Empire brought even grander developments to the Forum Romanum. Augustus, Rome's first emperor, undertook extensive renovations and new constructions to reflect his vision of a restored and glorified Rome. The Temple of Divus Julius, dedicated to the deified Julius Caesar, was built in the Forum, along with the Arch of Augustus, commemorating his military victories. Augustus also completed the Basilica Julia and added the Basilica Aemilia, further enhancing the Forum's role as a center of public life.

The Julio-Claudian emperors continued to enhance the Forum's grandeur. Tiberius built the Temple of Concord, symbolizing harmony between the Senate and the emperor. Caligula extended the Imperial Palace on the Palatine Hill to connect directly with the Forum, emphasizing the emperor's dominance over public and political life.

Claudius and Nero also contributed to the Forum's development, with Nero constructing the massive Domus Aurea (Golden House) nearby after the Great Fire of Rome in 64 CE.

The Flavian dynasty, which succeeded the Julio-Claudians, added new monumental structures to the Forum. Vespasian built the Temple of Peace, commemorating the end of the Jewish War, and his son Titus constructed the Arch of Titus, celebrating his victory in Jerusalem. The Arch of Titus is renowned for its detailed reliefs depicting the spoils of the Jewish Temple and the triumphal procession in Rome.

The Forum Romanum reached its architectural zenith under the emperors of the 2nd century CE. Trajan, known for his extensive building projects, constructed the Forum of Trajan, the largest and most elaborate of the imperial fora, adjacent to the Forum Romanum. This complex included the Basilica Ulpia, Trajan's Column, and a large marketplace. Trajan's successor, Hadrian, continued this legacy with the construction of the Temple of Venus and Roma, the largest temple in ancient Rome, located at the eastern edge of the Forum.

The Severan dynasty, which ruled in the late 2nd and early 3rd centuries CE, further embellished the Forum. Septimius Severus erected the Arch of Septimius Severus, celebrating his victories in the Parthian Wars. This arch, one of the best-preserved structures in the Forum, features intricate reliefs depicting scenes from his military campaigns. Caracalla, Severus' son, added the Temple of Serapis, a sanctuary for the Egyptian god, reflecting the growing influence of Eastern religions in Rome.

Despite its enduring significance, the Forum Romanum began to decline in the 3rd century CE as the Roman Empire faced increasing internal strife and external threats. The administrative and political focus gradually shifted to other parts of the city and the empire. The construction of the Aurelian Walls in the late 3rd century provided some protection, but Rome's importance as the center of the empire diminished as power moved to new imperial capitals like Constantinople.

The Forum Romanum suffered further damage during the invasions of the Goths in the 5th century CE and the subsequent fall of the Western Roman Empire. Many of its buildings were abandoned or repurposed, and the site gradually fell into disrepair. By the Middle Ages, the once-grand public space had transformed into a field of ruins, known as the "Campo Vaccino" or "Cow Field," as it was used for grazing livestock.

The Renaissance sparked renewed interest in the Forum Romanum as scholars and artists sought to rediscover and study the achievements of ancient Rome. Excavations and restorations began in earnest, revealing the Forum's buried treasures. The 19th and 20th centuries saw extensive archaeological work, uncovering and preserving many of the Forum's iconic structures. Today, the Forum Romanum is a protected archaeological site, open to visitors from around the world.

Walking through the ruins of the Forum Romanum today offers a profound connection to Rome's illustrious past. Visitors can explore the remains of the Temple of Saturn, with its towering columns; the Arch of Septimius Severus, with its detailed reliefs; the Curia Julia, where the Senate once convened; and the Basilica of Maxentius and Constantine, the largest structure in the Forum, showcasing the architectural prowess of late antiquity. Each ruin tells a story of political power, religious devotion, and civic life in ancient Rome.

The Forum Romanum's enduring legacy lies in its embodiment of Roman civilization's achievements and its influence on subsequent generations. It was the stage for many of Rome's most significant historical events, from Julius Caesar's assassination to the triumphal parades of victorious generals. The Forum's architectural and artistic contributions have inspired countless buildings and public spaces throughout history, reflecting the enduring impact of Roman culture.

Chapter 34: The Great Mosque of Djenné

The Great Mosque of Djenné, located in the town of Djenné in central Mali, is one of the most renowned and striking examples of Sudano-Sahelian architecture. This architectural masterpiece, constructed entirely from sun-baked earth bricks (adobe), plastered with a smooth mud coating, stands as a testament to the ingenuity and craftsmanship of the West African people. The mosque is not only a significant religious site but also a cultural and historical symbol, representing the rich heritage of the Mali Empire and its legacy.

The origins of the Great Mosque of Djenné can be traced back to the 13th century, during the reign of the Mali Empire, a powerful and wealthy state that controlled vast territories in West Africa. Djenné, situated along the Niger River, was a crucial center of trade, commerce, and Islamic scholarship. It served as a hub for the trans-Saharan trade routes, connecting sub-Saharan Africa with North Africa and the Mediterranean world. Goods such as gold, salt, and ivory were traded, and Djenné became a melting pot of cultures and ideas.

The first Great Mosque of Djenné was constructed around 1240 by the local king, Koi Konboro, who converted to Islam and made Djenné a center of Islamic learning and culture. This initial structure, however, was demolished in 1834 by Amadou Lobbo, the leader of the Massina Empire, during his jihad against what he considered unorthodox Islamic practices. The current mosque, which stands today, was rebuilt in 1907, under the direction of French colonial authorities, who aimed to restore and preserve the architectural heritage of the region.

The Great Mosque of Djenné is renowned for its unique and imposing architecture. The building's design incorporates elements of traditional West African building techniques and Islamic architectural influences, resulting in a distinctive and harmonious blend. The mosque is approximately 75 meters long and 40 meters wide, with its towering minarets reaching up to 16 meters in height, making it the largest mud-brick building in the world.

The most striking feature of the mosque is its three large minarets, which dominate the facade. These minarets are topped with ostrich eggs, symbolizing fertility and purity. The mosque's walls are adorned with wooden beams, known as torons, which protrude from the structure and serve both decorative and functional purposes. The torons provide support for scaffolding, allowing for the annual maintenance of the building. This maintenance is crucial, as the mud structure is susceptible to erosion and damage from the elements, particularly during the rainy season.

The interior of the mosque is equally impressive, with its large prayer hall capable of accommodating thousands of worshippers. The hall is supported by a network of pillars, creating a forest of columns that enhances the sense of space and grandeur. The roof is punctuated by small openings that allow natural light to filter in, creating a serene and contemplative atmosphere. The floors are covered with mats made from local reeds, providing a comfortable and natural surface for prayer.

One of the most significant aspects of the Great Mosque of Djenné is the annual maintenance event known as the "Crepissage," or plastering festival. This communal effort involves the entire community of Djenné, who come together to repair and re-plaster the mosque's walls. The Crepissage is a festive and vibrant occasion, marked by music, dance, and feasting. The event not only ensures the preservation of the mosque but also reinforces social cohesion and a sense of collective identity among the people of Djenné.

The Great Mosque of Djenné is more than just a place of worship; it is a center of learning and a symbol of the town's historical significance as a hub of Islamic scholarship. Djenné has long been associated with the transmission of Islamic knowledge, and the mosque played a central role in this intellectual tradition. Scholars from across

West Africa traveled to Djenné to study Islamic theology, jurisprudence, and the Arabic language. The town's numerous madrasas, or Islamic schools, contributed to the spread of Islam and the development of a learned and literate elite.

The architectural and cultural significance of the Great Mosque of Djenné has been recognized globally. In 1988, the mosque and the Old Towns of Djenné were designated as a UNESCO World Heritage Site. This recognition underscores the importance of the site as a testament to human creativity and cultural exchange. The mosque's construction techniques and design principles have inspired architects and scholars worldwide, contributing to a greater appreciation of West African architectural heritage.

Despite its grandeur and historical importance, the Great Mosque of Djenné faces several challenges. The structure's reliance on mud bricks makes it vulnerable to environmental factors, such as heavy rains and fluctuating temperatures, which can cause erosion and structural damage. Additionally, political instability and security concerns in Mali have impacted the preservation efforts and accessibility of the site. Nevertheless, local and international organizations continue to work towards safeguarding this invaluable cultural treasure.

The Great Mosque of Djenné also holds a special place in the hearts of the local community. It is a source of pride and identity for the people of Djenné, who view the mosque as a symbol of their history, faith, and resilience. The mosque's construction and maintenance have always been communal endeavors, reflecting the strong sense of cooperation and solidarity among the residents. The Crepissage festival, in particular, exemplifies this communal spirit, bringing together people of all ages and backgrounds in a shared effort to preserve their heritage.

The town of Djenné itself is a living museum, with its narrow streets, traditional mud-brick houses, and bustling markets offering a glimpse into a way of life that has persisted for centuries. The architectural style of the town's buildings, characterized by their thick mud walls and wooden torons, mirrors that of the Great Mosque, creating a cohesive and harmonious urban landscape. Djenné's rich history, vibrant culture, and architectural beauty continue to attract visitors, scholars, and researchers from around the world.

In recent years, efforts have been made to enhance the preservation and accessibility of the Great Mosque of Djenné. Initiatives include the training of local artisans in traditional building techniques, the establishment of conservation programs, and the promotion of sustainable tourism. These efforts aim to ensure that the mosque and its surrounding environment are protected for future generations, while also providing economic opportunities for the local community.

Chapter 35: Jericho

Jericho, often referred to as the "City of Palms," is one of the oldest continuously inhabited cities in the world, with a history that stretches back thousands of years. Situated in the Jordan Valley, near the Jordan River in the West Bank, Jericho is a city that has witnessed the rise and fall of numerous civilizations and has been a crucial crossroads of culture, trade, and politics throughout its extensive history.

The earliest known settlements in Jericho date back to around 10,000 BCE during the Neolithic period. Archaeological excavations at Tell es-Sultan, the ancient site of Jericho, have uncovered evidence of a pre-pottery Neolithic settlement that existed between 8500 and 7000 BCE. This period, often referred to as Pre-Pottery Neolithic A (PPNA), marks one of the first instances of organized, sedentary communities in human history. The inhabitants of Jericho during this time were among the first to practice agriculture, cultivating crops such as wheat and barley and domesticating animals like sheep and goats.

One of the most remarkable features of ancient Jericho from the PPNA period is the construction of a massive stone wall, which is considered one of the earliest known fortification systems in the world. This wall, accompanied by a large stone tower, likely served both defensive and ceremonial purposes. The presence of such sophisticated architecture indicates a highly organized society with the ability to mobilize labor and resources for large-scale construction projects. The wall and tower also suggest that Jericho was a significant settlement with potential threats that necessitated defensive structures.

As time progressed into the Pre-Pottery Neolithic B (PPNB) period (around 7000 to 5500 BCE), Jericho continued to grow and develop. During this era, the settlement expanded, and the use of mud bricks for building became more prevalent. The inhabitants of Jericho built rectangular houses with plastered floors, a marked advancement in architectural techniques. The city's population likely increased due to its strategic location and its role as a center for trade and agriculture.

Jericho's prominence continued into the Bronze Age, beginning around 3000 BCE. The city became a significant Canaanite urban center, known for its prosperity and strategic importance. During this period, Jericho was surrounded by a new set of massive walls, reflecting its continued need for defense and its status as a fortified city. The city-state of Jericho played a vital role in the network of Canaanite city-states, engaging in trade with neighboring regions and contributing to the cultural and economic development of the area.

The biblical account of Jericho, found in the Book of Joshua, describes the city's conquest by the Israelites led by Joshua. According to the narrative, the Israelites marched around the city's walls for seven days, and on the seventh day, the walls miraculously collapsed, allowing them to capture the city. While the historicity of this account is debated among scholars, the story of Jericho's fall has become an integral part of Judeo-Christian tradition and has contributed to the city's enduring legacy.

In the Iron Age, Jericho continued to be an important settlement, although it experienced periods of decline and revival. The city was part of the Kingdom of Israel and later the Kingdom of Judah. Throughout these periods, Jericho remained a vital agricultural and trade center, benefiting from its fertile land and abundant water sources from the nearby spring of Ein es-Sultan, also known as Elisha's Spring.

During the Hellenistic period (332-63 BCE), following the conquests of Alexander the Great, Jericho came under the influence of Greek culture and administration. The city was rebuilt and expanded, and its strategic location continued to attract settlers and traders. The construction of aqueducts and other infrastructure improvements during this time contributed to the city's prosperity.

The Roman period (63 BCE-324 CE) marked a significant era in the history of Jericho. The city became part of the Roman province of Judea and was known for its lush gardens, palaces, and a thriving date palm industry. Herod the Great, the Roman client king of Judea, constructed a winter palace in Jericho, complete with luxurious amenities, including a hippodrome and elaborate gardens. Herod's investments in Jericho transformed the city into a center of opulence and leisure, attracting the Roman elite.

The Byzantine period (324-638 CE) saw Jericho continue to flourish as a significant Christian center. Several churches and monasteries were built in and around the city, serving as places of worship and pilgrimage. The Monastery of Saint George, located in the nearby Wadi Qelt, is a notable example of Byzantine monastic architecture and remains an important religious site to this day.

Jericho's fortunes fluctuated during the early Islamic period (638-1099 CE), but the city remained a vital agricultural center. The Umayyad Caliphs recognized the strategic and economic importance of Jericho and invested in its development. The construction of the Hisham's Palace, an Umayyad residential complex, is a testament to the city's continued significance. The palace, with its intricate mosaics and elaborate architecture, reflects the cultural and artistic achievements of the Umayyad period.

The Crusader period (1099-1187 CE) saw Jericho come under the control of the Crusader Kingdom of Jerusalem. The city's agricultural productivity and strategic location continued to be valued by its rulers. However, the Crusaders' influence in Jericho was relatively short-lived, and the city eventually fell to the Muslim forces led by Saladin.

During the Mamluk period (1250-1517 CE), Jericho experienced a period of relative decline, although it remained an important agricultural center. The Mamluks built a number of structures in the region, including the Qasr al-Yahud, a site on the Jordan River associated with the baptism of Jesus. This site remains a significant pilgrimage destination for Christians.

The Ottoman period (1517-1917 CE) brought new developments to Jericho. The Ottomans constructed several public buildings and improved the city's infrastructure. Jericho's agricultural productivity continued to thrive, with the cultivation of dates, bananas, and other crops. The city's population remained relatively small but stable, and its strategic location ensured its continued importance.

In the 20th century, Jericho became part of the British Mandate of Palestine following World War I. The city witnessed significant changes during this period, including infrastructure improvements and population growth. The establishment of the State of Israel in 1948 and the subsequent Arab-Israeli conflict impacted Jericho, leading to periods of tension and displacement.

Following the Six-Day War in 1967, Jericho came under Israeli occupation. The Oslo Accords of the 1990s resulted in the transfer of administrative control of Jericho to the Palestinian Authority, and the city has since been part of the autonomous territories governed by the Palestinians.

Today, Jericho is a vibrant city that continues to attract visitors from around the world. Its rich history, archaeological sites, and cultural heritage make it a significant destination for tourists and scholars alike. The ancient site of Tell es-Sultan remains a focal point of archaeological research, offering insights into the early development of urban societies. The city's numerous historical landmarks, including Hisham's Palace, the Monastery of Saint George, and the Qasr al-Yahud, provide a tangible connection to its storied past.

Jericho's modern development has also been marked by efforts to preserve and promote its cultural heritage. Initiatives to restore and protect archaeological sites, improve infrastructure, and promote sustainable tourism aim to ensure that Jericho's historical legacy is preserved for future generations. The city's agricultural sector, particularly the cultivation of dates, bananas, and citrus fruits, continues to play a vital role in its economy.

Chapter 36: Çatalhöyük

Çatalhöyük, located in modern-day Turkey, is one of the most significant archaeological sites in the world, providing an unparalleled glimpse into early human urban life. This Neolithic settlement, which flourished between approximately 7500 and 5700 BCE, is renowned for its unique layout, advanced societal organization, and rich cultural artifacts. It stands as one of the best-preserved examples of early agricultural society and offers profound insights into the lives of our ancient ancestors.

The discovery of Çatalhöyük in the early 1960s by British archaeologist James Mellaart marked a turning point in our understanding of Neolithic civilization. The site is situated in the Konya Plain in south-central Turkey, covering an area of about 13 hectares. The settlement is characterized by its densely packed, honeycomb-like structure of mud-brick houses, which were built directly adjacent to one another without streets or alleyways. This architectural style necessitated that residents used the rooftops and ladders to move between homes and different parts of the settlement, effectively creating a vertical village.

The homes of Çatalhöyük were rectangular and featured flat roofs, which played a significant role in daily life, serving as communal spaces for social interaction, food preparation, and various domestic activities. The walls of these houses were often plastered and painted, displaying elaborate murals and decorations that depicted hunting scenes, geometric designs, and symbolic imagery. These artistic expressions provide valuable insights into the spiritual and cultural world of Çatalhöyük's inhabitants.

One of the most striking aspects of Çatalhöyük is its egalitarian social structure. Unlike many later civilizations, there is little evidence of significant social stratification or centralized authority. The uniformity in the size and construction of houses suggests a relatively equal distribution of wealth and resources among the population. The absence of large public buildings or palaces further supports the notion of an egalitarian society. This challenges earlier assumptions that hierarchical social structures were necessary for the development of urban life.

The economy of Çatalhöyük was primarily based on agriculture, supplemented by hunting and gathering. The fertile plains surrounding the settlement allowed for the cultivation of a variety of crops, including wheat, barley, peas, and lentils. The domestication of animals, such as sheep, goats, and cattle, played a crucial role in the community's sustenance and economic activities. The presence of various agricultural tools, such as sickles and grinding stones, highlights the advanced farming techniques employed by the inhabitants.

Trade also played a vital role in Çatalhöyük's economy. Archaeological evidence indicates that the settlement engaged in long-distance trade with neighboring regions, exchanging goods such as obsidian, shells, and pottery. The presence of obsidian, a volcanic glass prized for its sharp edges, suggests that Çatalhöyük was a significant center for the production and trade of this valuable material. The exchange of goods facilitated cultural interactions and the dissemination of ideas, contributing to the settlement's development and prosperity.

Religion and ritual practices were integral to life in Çatalhöyük. The settlement is renowned for its numerous shrines and religious artifacts, indicating a complex spiritual belief system. Many houses contained special rooms or areas dedicated to religious practices, featuring altars, figurines, and symbolic decorations. The famous "mother goddess" figurines, found in various parts of the site, are believed to represent fertility and the earth's abundance, highlighting the community's reverence for nature and its cycles.

Burial practices at Çatalhöyük were unique and provide further insight into the spiritual beliefs of its inhabitants. People were often buried beneath the floors of their homes, a practice that suggests a close connection between the living and the dead. The deceased were typically placed in a fetal position, sometimes accompanied by grave goods such as tools, ornaments, and food offerings. This practice indicates a belief in an afterlife and the continuation of familial and communal ties beyond death.

The intricate murals and reliefs found within the homes of Çatalhöyük are among the most remarkable features of the site. These artworks, which include scenes of hunting, wildlife, and symbolic motifs, provide a window into the cognitive and artistic expressions of Neolithic people. The depiction of hunting scenes, despite evidence that agriculture was the primary subsistence strategy, suggests the importance of hunting as a cultural and symbolic activity. These artistic works also highlight the community's deep connection to the natural world and its inhabitants.

Çatalhöyük's significance extends beyond its material culture and architecture. The site has provided invaluable information about the social, economic, and religious practices of early agricultural societies. The absence of clear social hierarchies, the communal nature of its architecture, and the rich symbolic and ritual life all contribute to our understanding of the diversity and complexity of Neolithic societies. Çatalhöyük challenges the notion that urbanization and social complexity necessarily lead to hierarchical and stratified societies, offering an alternative model of early human urban life.

The preservation and excavation of Çatalhöyük have been the focus of extensive archaeological efforts. Since its discovery, numerous international teams have worked on the site, employing advanced technologies and methodologies to uncover its secrets. The use of techniques such as ground-penetrating radar, 3D modeling, and microarchaeology has allowed researchers to gain a more comprehensive understanding of the settlement's layout, construction methods, and daily activities.

The Çatalhöyük Research Project, initiated in the 1990s and led by archaeologist Ian Hodder, has been particularly influential in advancing our knowledge of the site. This project has emphasized a multidisciplinary approach, incorporating perspectives from archaeology, anthropology, environmental science, and other fields to create a holistic picture of life at Çatalhöyük. The project has also prioritized the preservation and conservation of the site, ensuring that it remains a valuable resource for future generations of researchers and the public.

Çatalhöyük has also played a significant role in discussions about the origins and development of urbanization. As one of the earliest known examples of a proto-city, it provides critical evidence for the processes that led to the rise of complex urban societies. The settlement's unique layout, with its densely packed houses and lack of streets, challenges traditional definitions of a city and prompts reevaluation of what constitutes urban living. Çatalhöyük's example suggests that urbanization can take multiple forms and that early urban societies were diverse in their organization and structure.

The cultural and historical importance of Çatalhöyük has been recognized internationally. In 2012, the site was designated as a UNESCO World Heritage Site, highlighting its outstanding universal value as an exceptional testimony to a cultural tradition and an important stage in human history. This recognition underscores the need to protect and preserve Çatalhöyük for its archaeological significance and its contribution to our understanding of early human societies.

Public interest in Çatalhöyük has grown significantly, with the site attracting scholars, students, and tourists from around the world. Educational programs and visitor facilities have been developed to enhance public engagement and appreciation of the site. The Çatalhöyük Visitor Center, opened in 2005, provides informative displays, interactive exhibits, and guided tours that allow visitors to explore the site and learn about its history and significance.

Chapter 37: Temple of Artemis

The Temple of Artemis, also known as the Artemision, was a grand and magnificent structure dedicated to the Greek goddess Artemis. It was located in the ancient city of Ephesus, which is near the modern town of Selçuk in present-day Turkey. The temple is one of the Seven Wonders of the Ancient World, renowned for its extraordinary size, architectural beauty, and artistic splendor. Its history spans several centuries, marked by multiple reconstructions and significant cultural and religious influence.

The origins of the Temple of Artemis date back to around 800 BCE, when a smaller sanctuary was first built on the site. This early temple was relatively modest, but it laid the foundation for what would become one of the most celebrated religious edifices in antiquity. The goddess Artemis, worshiped as the deity of the hunt, wilderness, and fertility, held great importance in Ephesus and the surrounding regions. Her sanctuary attracted worshippers from far and wide, contributing to the city's status as a major religious center.

The temple's most famous incarnation, often referred to as the Great Temple of Artemis, began construction around 550 BCE. This monumental project was initiated by the wealthy Lydian king Croesus, who sought to create a structure that would reflect the magnificence and power of his kingdom. The design of the temple was entrusted to the Greek architect Chersiphron and his son Metagenes. The construction process was a colossal undertaking, involving skilled artisans, laborers, and vast resources.

The Great Temple of Artemis was an exemplary model of classical Greek architecture, featuring the Ionic order. It measured approximately 115 meters in length and 55 meters in width, making it the largest temple of its time. The structure was supported by 127 marble columns, each standing around 18 meters tall. These columns were intricately carved and adorned with exquisite reliefs, showcasing the artistic mastery of the period. The temple's design incorporated a double row of columns on all four sides, creating a grand colonnade that emphasized its monumental scale and aesthetic harmony.

One of the most striking features of the Temple of Artemis was its opulent decoration. The pediments, friezes, and metopes were adorned with elaborate sculptures depicting scenes from Greek mythology and the life of Artemis. These artworks were crafted by some of the finest sculptors of the era, including Scopas and Phidias. The central statue of Artemis, housed within the temple's inner sanctum, was a masterpiece in itself. This statue, made of gold and ivory, depicted the goddess in her role as a protector of women and children, adorned with intricate jewelry and holding symbols of her divine attributes.

The temple served not only as a religious sanctuary but also as a hub of cultural and economic activity. It was a place of pilgrimage for worshippers who came to offer sacrifices, seek blessings, and participate in various religious festivals. The annual festival of Artemis, known as the Artemisia, attracted thousands of visitors, including dignitaries, merchants, and travelers. This festival featured grand processions, athletic competitions, music, dance, and theatrical performances, highlighting the temple's role as a center of communal and cultural life.

The Temple of Artemis also played a significant role in the economic prosperity of Ephesus. It served as a depository for vast amounts of wealth, including donations from wealthy patrons, offerings from worshippers, and revenues from trade. The temple's treasury became one of the most secure and respected financial institutions in the ancient world, attracting deposits from individuals and states alike. This economic influence extended beyond Ephesus, enhancing the city's status as a major trading hub and contributing to its overall prosperity.

Despite its grandeur and significance, the Temple of Artemis faced numerous challenges and calamities throughout its history. In 356 BCE, the temple was destroyed by a fire set by Herostratus, a man seeking notoriety. This act of arson caused immense devastation, reducing the magnificent structure to ruins. However, the Ephesians were determined to rebuild their beloved temple, and construction of a new, even more magnificent temple began shortly after the destruction. This reconstruction effort involved the collective contributions of the citizens of Ephesus, as well as financial support from Alexander the Great, who visited the site and offered to fund the project.

The new Temple of Artemis, completed around 323 BCE, retained the grandeur and splendor of its predecessor. The design remained faithful to the original, with some enhancements and refinements. The temple continued to serve as a major religious and cultural center, attracting worshippers and visitors from across the ancient world. However, it faced further challenges, including damage from earthquakes and plundering by various invaders.

The decline of the Temple of Artemis began in the late Roman period, as the rise of Christianity led to a gradual erosion of traditional pagan worship. In 262 CE, the temple suffered severe damage during a raid by the Goths. The final blow came in 401 CE when it was destroyed by a Christian mob led by the archbishop of Constantinople, John Chrysostom, who sought to eradicate pagan symbols and temples. The remains of the temple were gradually dismantled, and its stones were repurposed for other construction projects.

Today, only the foundations and a few scattered fragments of the Temple of Artemis remain at the archaeological site of Ephesus. Despite its physical absence, the legacy of the temple endures through historical accounts, artistic depictions, and the enduring fascination it inspires. The Temple of Artemis stands as a testament to the architectural and artistic achievements of ancient civilizations, as well as the complex interplay of religion, culture, and politics in shaping human history.

The study and excavation of the Temple of Artemis have provided invaluable insights into the architectural techniques, artistic styles, and religious practices of the ancient world. Archaeologists and historians continue to explore the site and its surroundings, uncovering artifacts and remnants that shed light on the daily life, beliefs, and interactions of the people who once worshipped at this magnificent sanctuary. The temple's inclusion as one of the Seven Wonders of the Ancient World underscores its significance and enduring impact on human civilization.

The Temple of Artemis also holds a place in the broader narrative of cultural exchange and interaction in the ancient Mediterranean. Its construction and decoration reflect the influence of various cultures, including Greek, Lydian, Persian, and Egyptian. The temple's location in Ephesus, a bustling port city, facilitated the exchange of ideas, goods, and artistic traditions, making it a melting pot of diverse influences. This cultural amalgamation is evident in the temple's architectural features, artistic motifs, and religious practices, highlighting the interconnectedness of ancient civilizations.

In modern times, the Temple of Artemis continues to captivate scholars, artists, and tourists alike. The site of Ephesus attracts millions of visitors each year, drawn by the allure of its ancient ruins and the stories they tell. Efforts to preserve and protect the site are ongoing, ensuring that future generations can appreciate and learn from this remarkable testament to human ingenuity and devotion.

Chapter 38: The Olmec Heads

The Olmec civilization, which thrived in the tropical lowlands of south-central Mexico, is one of the earliest known Mesoamerican cultures, flourishing approximately between 1200 and 400 BCE. Among their most extraordinary and enigmatic legacies are the colossal stone heads, known as the Olmec heads. These monumental sculptures, each weighing several tons, are a remarkable testament to the artistic and engineering prowess of the Olmec people. The Olmec heads not only reflect the complexity of Olmec society but also provide significant insights into their cultural, religious, and political life.

The discovery of the Olmec heads has been one of the most fascinating chapters in the history of archaeology. The first of these heads was unearthed in the early 19th century, but it wasn't until the 20th century that their significance began to be fully understood. To date, seventeen heads have been found, primarily in the states of Veracruz and Tabasco. The largest of these heads, discovered at the site of La Cobata, measures nearly ten feet in height and weighs around 40 tons. Each head is distinct, with unique facial features, suggesting that they may represent individual rulers or important figures within Olmec society.

The creation of these colossal heads required extraordinary effort and ingenuity. The stone used for the heads, basalt, was not locally available in the Olmec heartland. Instead, it had to be quarried from distant mountains, sometimes transported over 50 miles. This process would have involved a large, coordinated workforce and sophisticated logistical planning. Once the massive stone blocks arrived at their destination, skilled artisans would carve them using rudimentary tools made from harder stones like jadeite and obsidian. The precision and detail of the carvings, especially considering the scale and hardness of the basalt, are truly remarkable.

The exact purpose and significance of the Olmec heads remain a subject of ongoing debate among scholars. One widely accepted theory is that the heads represent Olmec rulers, immortalizing their visages in stone. The detailed and individualized features of each head support this idea, as they suggest a focus on capturing specific likenesses rather than creating generalized or idealized images. The heads may have served as powerful symbols of authority and continuity, reinforcing the ruler's divine right to govern and maintaining social cohesion within Olmec communities.

The headdresses depicted on the heads are another intriguing aspect, often elaborately adorned and differing from one sculpture to the next. These headdresses could indicate rank, status, or even specific roles within the society. They might also have religious or ceremonial significance, linking the rulers to the divine or to specific deities worshipped by the Olmec. Some scholars propose that the heads were placed in strategic locations, such as ceremonial centers or along processional routes, to underscore the ruler's presence and power throughout the territory.

The Olmec heads also provide valuable clues about the broader cultural and artistic context of the Olmec civilization. The style and craftsmanship of the heads show a high degree of sophistication, indicating that the Olmec had well-developed artistic traditions and skilled artisans. The emphasis on portraiture and the ability to capture distinct facial features suggest a complex society with an interest in individual identity and status. Additionally, the Olmec heads reflect a broader Mesoamerican tradition of monumental sculpture, linking the Olmec to later cultures such as the Maya and the Aztecs, who also created large-scale stone carvings to commemorate rulers and deities.

The locations where the Olmec heads have been found offer important insights into the geographic and social landscape of the Olmec civilization. Major Olmec sites like San Lorenzo, La Venta, and Tres Zapotes have yielded multiple heads, indicating that these were significant centers of political and ceremonial activity. The distribution of the heads suggests a network of interconnected communities, each contributing to and benefiting from the broader cultural and religious practices of the Olmec world. These sites also provide evidence of complex urban planning, with ceremonial platforms, plazas, and other monumental structures that reflect the organized and hierarchical nature of Olmec society.

The discovery and study of the Olmec heads have also highlighted the importance of interdisciplinary approaches in archaeology. Advances in technology, such as 3D scanning and digital modeling, have allowed researchers to analyze the heads in unprecedented detail, revealing new information about their construction, transport, and placement. Geological studies have traced the origin of the basalt used in the heads, shedding light on the extensive trade and transport networks that existed in ancient Mesoamerica. Additionally, ongoing excavations and research continue to uncover new aspects of Olmec life, providing a more comprehensive understanding of this influential civilization.

Despite the significant progress made in understanding the Olmec heads, many questions remain unanswered. The lack of written records from the Olmec period means that much of what we know is based on interpretation of the archaeological evidence. The symbolic meanings of the heads, the exact nature of the political and religious systems that produced them, and the daily lives of the people who created and venerated these sculptures are still subjects of speculation and research. The Olmec heads continue to be a focal point for scholarly debate and inquiry, embodying both the achievements and the mysteries of one of Mesoamerica's earliest civilizations.

The legacy of the Olmec heads extends beyond their historical and archaeological significance. They have become iconic symbols of Mexico's pre-Columbian heritage, representing the ingenuity, creativity, and complexity of ancient Mesoamerican societies. The heads are featured prominently in museums and exhibitions around the world, helping to educate and inspire people about the rich cultural traditions of the Olmec and their lasting impact on subsequent civilizations. Efforts to preserve and protect the Olmec heads and other archaeological sites are crucial for ensuring that future generations can continue to learn from and appreciate this remarkable cultural legacy.

In popular culture, the Olmec heads have also captured the imagination of artists, writers, and filmmakers, often depicted as enigmatic relics of a lost civilization. They appear in literature, film, and television, sometimes imbued with mystical or supernatural qualities. This fascination reflects a broader human interest in the ancient past and the desire to uncover and understand the mysteries of early human societies. The Olmec heads, with their imposing presence and enigmatic expressions, serve as powerful reminders of the complexity and diversity of human history.

Chapter 39: The Nasca Lines

The Nasca Lines, etched into the arid plains of the Peruvian desert, are among the most enigmatic and captivating archaeological wonders of the ancient world. Stretching across the Nazca Desert, these intricate geoglyphs cover an area of approximately 450 square kilometers (175 square miles) and include a variety of designs, ranging from simple lines and geometric shapes to elaborate depictions of animals, plants, and mythical beings. The Nasca Lines were created by the Nasca culture, which flourished in the region between 200 BCE and 600 CE. Despite extensive research, the precise purpose and meaning of the Nasca Lines remain subjects of ongoing debate and fascination.

The discovery of the Nasca Lines can be attributed to Peruvian archaeologist Toribio Mejía Xesspe, who first reported seeing them in the 1920s. However, it wasn't until the 1930s, when commercial flights began to pass over the region, that the full scale and complexity of the geoglyphs became apparent. The aerial perspective revealed a vast network of designs, some stretching over several kilometers, meticulously carved into the desert floor. This newfound visibility sparked a wave of scholarly interest and public intrigue, leading to numerous studies and theories about their origin and purpose.

The Nasca Lines are remarkable for their size, precision, and diversity. The simplest designs are straight lines that extend for kilometers, while more complex figures include spirals, trapezoids, and zigzags. The most famous geoglyphs, however, are the biomorphic figures, which depict various animals such as hummingbirds, spiders, monkeys, fish, and lizards, as well as human-like figures and fantastical creatures. These figures range in size from 50 to 300 meters (165 to 985 feet) in length, and their creation required an extraordinary degree of planning, coordination, and artistic skill.

The method used to create the Nasca Lines involved removing the top layer of reddish-brown iron oxide-coated pebbles to reveal the lighter-colored earth beneath. This process, known as "scraping," exposed the pale desert floor, creating a stark contrast that made the designs visible from a distance. The lines have remained remarkably well-preserved due to the dry, stable climate of the Nazca Desert, which experiences minimal rainfall and wind. This preservation has allowed modern researchers to study the geoglyphs in detail and gain insights into the techniques and tools used by the Nasca people.

One of the most enduring mysteries of the Nasca Lines is their purpose. Numerous theories have been proposed, ranging from astronomical markers and religious symbols to agricultural calendars and pathways for ceremonial processions. One prominent theory, advanced by German mathematician and archaeologist Maria Reiche, suggests that the lines functioned as a massive astronomical calendar. According to Reiche, the geoglyphs align with celestial events such as solstices and equinoxes, allowing the Nasca to track the movement of the sun, moon, and stars. This theory posits that the lines served both practical and ceremonial purposes, helping to regulate agricultural activities and religious observances.

Another theory, proposed by American archaeologist Paul Kosok and later supported by Reiche, is that the lines were used for ritual processions. The idea is that the Nasca people would walk along the paths of the geoglyphs as part of religious ceremonies, perhaps to honor deities associated with water and fertility. This theory is supported by the presence of pottery shards and other artifacts found along some of the lines, suggesting that offerings were made during these processions. The ceremonial use of the lines would also explain the creation of large, visually striking figures intended to be seen by participants walking the geoglyphs.

The Nasca Lines may also have had a symbolic or mythological significance. Some researchers argue that the geoglyphs represent sacred animals, plants, and deities central to Nasca cosmology and mythology. The large size and intricate detail of the figures suggest that they were created with great reverence and dedication, possibly as a means of invoking divine favor or ensuring cosmic harmony. This symbolic interpretation is reinforced by the Nasca's extensive knowledge of their natural environment and their ability to integrate their artistic expressions with the surrounding landscape.

In addition to these theories, some scholars propose that the Nasca Lines were related to water, a vital and scarce resource in the arid desert region. This theory, advanced by archaeologists such as Johan Reinhard, suggests that the geoglyphs were part of a complex system of rituals and practices designed to invoke rain and ensure agricultural fertility. The Nasca's reliance on irrigation and their sophisticated understanding of hydraulic engineering lend credence to the idea that the lines were connected to water management and ritualistic appeals for rain.

Modern technology has significantly advanced our understanding of the Nasca Lines. High-resolution satellite imagery, drone surveys, and ground-penetrating radar have allowed archaeologists to map the geoglyphs in unprecedented detail, revealing new figures and refining our knowledge of existing ones. These technologies have also helped identify the techniques and tools used to create the lines, as well as the cultural and environmental factors that influenced their design and preservation. Despite these advances, the Nasca Lines continue to pose many unanswered questions, and ongoing research aims to uncover more about the people who created them and the society they lived in.

The Nasca Lines are more than just an archaeological curiosity; they are a testament to the ingenuity, creativity, and spiritual depth of the Nasca culture. They reflect a sophisticated understanding of geometry, astronomy, and the natural world, as well as a profound connection to the landscape and the cosmos. The lines' enduring mystery and beauty continue to inspire awe and wonder, drawing visitors from around the world to the Peruvian desert.

Efforts to preserve and protect the Nasca Lines are crucial for ensuring that future generations can study and appreciate this extraordinary cultural heritage. The site was designated a UNESCO World Heritage Site in 1994, recognizing its global significance and the need for ongoing conservation. However, the Nasca Lines face threats from modern development, tourism, and environmental changes, necessitating careful management and protection.

Chapter 40: Ħaġar Qim

Ħaġar Qim, a prehistoric megalithic temple complex located on the island of Malta, is one of the most remarkable and ancient archaeological sites in the world. Dating back to the Ġgantija phase (3600-3200 BCE) of Maltese prehistory, Ħaġar Qim stands as a testament to the advanced engineering and artistic skills of its builders. The name Ħaġar Qim translates to "Standing Stones" in Maltese, reflecting the site's primary characteristic of large limestone megaliths arranged in a complex architectural layout. This ancient temple complex offers invaluable insights into the religious, cultural, and technological achievements of the early inhabitants of Malta.

The discovery of Ħaġar Qim dates back to 1839 when it was first documented during an excavation led by English artist and antiquarian Charles Frederick de Brocktorff. Since then, it has been the subject of numerous archaeological studies, revealing a wealth of information about the prehistoric Maltese society. The site consists of a series of interlinked structures, including the main temple and several ancillary buildings, all constructed using massive limestone blocks. Some of these blocks weigh several tons, and their precise placement highlights the sophisticated engineering capabilities of the builders.

One of the most striking features of Ħaġar Qim is the entrance to the main temple, marked by a trilithon, a structure consisting of two vertical stones supporting a third horizontal stone, creating a doorway. This entrance leads into a series of oval and circular chambers, interconnected by passageways and punctuated by altars, niches, and benches. The layout of the temple suggests a highly organized and symbolic architectural plan, likely reflecting the religious and ceremonial functions of the complex.

The architectural design of Ħaġar Qim includes several significant elements that provide clues about its construction and use. The walls of the temple are built using a combination of large upright stones and smaller, carefully fitted blocks, creating a sturdy and durable structure. The interior chambers often feature corbelled roofs, where stones are laid in overlapping layers to create a stable, dome-like ceiling. This technique indicates a sophisticated understanding of structural principles and the ability to manipulate heavy materials with precision.

One of the most intriguing aspects of Ħaġar Qim is the presence of various carved stone features, including altars, statues, and decorative motifs. These carvings often depict abstract patterns, such as spirals, dots, and chevrons, which may have held symbolic or ritual significance. The site also includes several freestanding statues, known as "fat lady" figurines, representing corpulent female figures. These statues are thought to symbolize fertility and abundance, reflecting the temple's possible role as a center for fertility rites and agricultural rituals.

Ħaġar Qim's location on a hilltop overlooking the Mediterranean Sea further emphasizes its significance. The temple's orientation and alignment suggest that it may have been designed to capture and utilize natural light, particularly during the solstices and equinoxes. Some researchers propose that the temple's entrance and main chamber were aligned to allow sunlight to illuminate specific areas during these celestial events, possibly marking important times in the agricultural calendar or religious observances.

The site also includes several large, perforated stones, known as "oracle holes" or "oracle stones," which may have been used for divination or communication with the divine. These stones are strategically placed within the temple complex, suggesting that they played a crucial role in the rituals and ceremonies conducted at Ħaġar Qim. The presence of these features highlights the temple's function as a sacred space, where the community could engage with spiritual and supernatural forces.

The construction of Ħaġar Qim and other megalithic temples on Malta required significant social organization, resource management, and technical skill. The builders would have needed to quarry, transport, and precisely place the massive limestone blocks, a feat that likely involved coordinated labor and advanced knowledge of engineering principles. The creation of such an elaborate and enduring structure suggests that the society that built Ħaġar Qim was highly organized and capable of mobilizing substantial resources for religious and ceremonial purposes.

Archaeological excavations at Ħaġar Qim have uncovered a variety of artifacts, including pottery, stone tools, and animal bones, which provide further insights into the daily life and practices of the temple's builders and users. The pottery found at the site is often decorated with intricate patterns and motifs, indicating a developed artistic tradition. The presence of animal bones suggests that feasting and offerings were an integral part of the rituals conducted at the temple, possibly involving the sacrifice of livestock to appease the gods or ensure agricultural fertility.

The significance of Ħaġar Qim extends beyond its architectural and artistic achievements. The temple complex provides crucial evidence about the religious beliefs and social organization of the prehistoric Maltese people. The construction and use of such a monumental structure indicate a society with complex spiritual and ceremonial practices, likely involving a priestly or elite class responsible for overseeing religious activities. The emphasis on fertility and abundance, as reflected in the carvings and figurines, suggests that the temple played a central role in the community's efforts to ensure agricultural success and prosperity.

In addition to its historical and cultural importance, Ħaġar Qim has faced various challenges related to preservation and conservation. The site has been exposed to natural elements for thousands of years, resulting in weathering and erosion of the limestone structures. Efforts to protect and preserve Ħaġar Qim have included the construction of a protective shelter to shield the temple from rain, wind, and direct sunlight. These measures are essential for ensuring the long-term survival of the site and allowing future generations to study and appreciate this remarkable testament to human ingenuity and spirituality.

Ħaġar Qim, along with other megalithic temples on Malta, has been recognized as a UNESCO World Heritage Site, highlighting its global significance and the need for ongoing conservation efforts. The site's inclusion on the World Heritage list underscores the importance of preserving such ancient monuments, which provide invaluable insights into the early history of human civilization and the development of complex societies.

The study of Ħaġar Qim and other megalithic temples continues to evolve, with new discoveries and technological advancements shedding light on the mysteries of these ancient structures. Modern techniques, such as ground-penetrating radar and 3D scanning, have allowed researchers to explore the site in greater detail, uncovering hidden features and gaining a deeper understanding of its construction and use. These ongoing efforts contribute to a more comprehensive understanding of the prehistoric Maltese culture and the remarkable achievements of its people.

Chapter 41: Mount Nemrut

Mount Nemrut, located in southeastern Turkey, is one of the most remarkable archaeological sites in the world. Standing at 2,134 meters (7,001 feet) above sea level, this mountain is renowned for its ancient monumental statues and royal tomb, which date back to the first century BCE. The site is the tomb sanctuary of King Antiochus I Theos of Commagene, a small Hellenistic kingdom that existed in the region from the second century BCE to the first century CE. The construction of this extraordinary complex reflects the cultural and political aspirations of Antiochus and his kingdom, blending elements of Greek, Persian, and local Anatolian traditions.

The history of Mount Nemrut is closely tied to the Kingdom of Commagene, which was located in the region that today encompasses parts of southeastern Turkey. Antiochus I Theos, who reigned from approximately 70 to 36 BCE, was a king of mixed Greek and Persian ancestry. He sought to legitimize and glorify his rule by creating a monumental sanctuary on the summit of Mount Nemrut, which would serve as both a tomb and a place of worship. The site was intended to honor not only himself but also the gods and ancestors of his diverse cultural heritage.

The most striking feature of Mount Nemrut is the series of colossal statues that once adorned the site. These statues, which originally stood up to 10 meters (33 feet) high, include depictions of various gods, as well as Antiochus himself. The statues were carved from local limestone and were seated on thrones, arranged in a specific order along the east and west terraces of the sanctuary. The gods represented include Zeus-Oromasdes (a syncretic deity combining elements of the Greek god Zeus and the Persian god Ahura Mazda), Hercules-Artagnes (a fusion of the Greek hero Hercules and the Persian god Verethragna), and Apollo-Mithras-Helios-Hermes (a composite deity combining aspects of the Greek gods Apollo and Hermes with the Persian god Mithra).

In addition to the statues of the gods, the sanctuary features the impressive statue of Antiochus himself, portrayed as a divine figure seated among the gods. This self-deification was a common practice among Hellenistic rulers, who sought to legitimize their authority by associating themselves with divine figures. The presence of Antiochus's statue among the gods emphasizes his aspirations to be remembered as a god-king, bridging the gap between the human and divine realms.

The statues at Mount Nemrut are accompanied by large stone heads that have fallen from their bodies over the centuries. These heads, scattered across the terraces, have become iconic symbols of the site. Despite their detached state, the heads remain remarkably well-preserved, allowing visitors to appreciate the detailed craftsmanship and artistic skill of the ancient sculptors. The expressive faces of the statues, with their distinct features and elaborate headdresses, reflect a blend of Greek and Persian artistic influences, characteristic of the syncretic culture of Commagene.

The sanctuary at Mount Nemrut is divided into three main terraces: the east terrace, the west terrace, and the north terrace. The east and west terraces are the primary locations of the colossal statues and are thought to have been the main ceremonial areas of the sanctuary. The east terrace features a well-preserved arrangement of statues, stone reliefs, and an altar, which may have been used for sacrificial offerings. The west terrace, while similar in layout, is less well-preserved but still provides valuable insights into the religious practices and artistic achievements of the ancient Commagenians.

One of the most intriguing aspects of Mount Nemrut is the complex and detailed astronomical alignments of the sanctuary. The layout of the statues and the overall design of the site suggest that it was carefully planned to align with certain celestial events. Some scholars propose that the sanctuary functioned as an astronomical observatory, with specific alignments corresponding to the solstices, equinoxes, and other significant celestial occurrences. This astronomical aspect of

Mount Nemrut highlights the advanced knowledge and scientific interests of the ancient Commagenians, as well as their desire to connect their religious practices with the cosmos.

Inscriptions found at the site provide further insights into the religious and political significance of Mount Nemrut. These inscriptions, carved into the stone in Greek and Aramaic, include dedicatory texts, decrees, and prayers composed by Antiochus himself. They reveal the king's intentions for the sanctuary, his religious beliefs, and his efforts to immortalize his legacy. The inscriptions emphasize themes of divine favor, eternal glory, and the unity of different cultural traditions, reflecting Antiochus's vision of a harmonious and syncretic kingdom.

The construction of the sanctuary at Mount Nemrut was an enormous undertaking that required significant resources and labor. The site is thought to have been built over several decades, involving the quarrying and transportation of massive limestone blocks up the steep slopes of the mountain. The logistics of this construction project, including the precise carving and placement of the statues and the creation of the terraces, demonstrate the impressive engineering capabilities of the ancient Commagenians. The sheer scale and ambition of the project reflect Antiochus's determination to create a lasting monument to his reign and his religious beliefs.

Despite its ancient origins, Mount Nemrut remained relatively unknown to the outside world until the 19th century. The site was rediscovered in 1881 by Karl Sester, a German engineer conducting surveys for the Ottoman government. Sester's reports of the colossal statues and monumental tomb sparked international interest, leading to further exploration and excavation by archaeologists. The site has since been the focus of extensive research, conservation efforts, and tourism, becoming one of Turkey's most important cultural heritage sites.

Mount Nemrut's significance extends beyond its archaeological and historical value. The site has been recognized as a UNESCO World Heritage Site, highlighting its importance as a cultural and architectural marvel. Efforts to preserve and protect Mount Nemrut are crucial for ensuring that future generations can appreciate and study this extraordinary monument. The remote and rugged location of the site, combined with the challenges posed by weather and natural erosion, necessitates ongoing conservation measures to safeguard the statues and terraces from further deterioration.

Chapter 42: Mesa Verde

Mesa Verde, located in the southwestern region of Colorado, is one of the most significant and well-preserved archaeological sites in the United States. This remarkable location, designated as a National Park and a UNESCO World Heritage Site, offers a profound glimpse into the lives of the Ancestral Puebloans, also known as the Anasazi, who inhabited the area for over 700 years from approximately 600 to 1300 CE. Mesa Verde, which means "Green Table" in Spanish, encompasses more than 52,000 acres and is renowned for its well-preserved cliff dwellings, including the famous Cliff Palace, as well as numerous other structures and artifacts that provide insight into the ancient culture that thrived there.

The history of Mesa Verde can be divided into several distinct periods, reflecting the evolution of the Ancestral Puebloan culture over centuries. The earliest inhabitants of the region were hunter-gatherers who lived in simple pithouses. These semi-subterranean structures, built of wood and earth, were typically circular and had a central hearth. The Basketmaker period, which began around 600 CE, marked a significant transition as the people of Mesa Verde started to adopt a more sedentary lifestyle, relying increasingly on agriculture. Corn, beans, and squash became staple crops, and the population began to grow.

By 750 CE, the inhabitants of Mesa Verde had started to build above-ground structures known as pueblos. These early pueblos were constructed from stone and adobe and were often multi-roomed and multi-storied. The architectural advancements during this period were significant, with the development of kivas, which were ceremonial rooms used for religious and community gatherings. Kivas were typically circular and subterranean, reflecting the earlier pithouse designs but with more elaborate construction techniques.

The Classic period of Mesa Verde, which spanned from 900 to 1300 CE, saw the peak of Ancestral Puebloan culture in the region. During this time, the population expanded significantly, and the people constructed the iconic cliff dwellings for which Mesa Verde is renowned. These cliff dwellings, built into the alcoves of the canyon walls, provided both protection and shelter. The most famous of these dwellings, Cliff Palace, is the largest cliff dwelling in North America. It contains over 150 rooms and 23 kivas, indicating a highly organized and socially complex community.

The construction of the cliff dwellings at Mesa Verde required advanced architectural and engineering skills. The Ancestral Puebloans used sandstone blocks, which they meticulously shaped and fitted together with mortar made from a mixture of mud and water. The structures were built into natural alcoves, which provided natural protection from the elements and potential invaders. The placement of the dwellings also maximized solar exposure, allowing the inhabitants to take advantage of the sun's warmth during the winter months while remaining cool in the summer.

Life in the cliff dwellings of Mesa Verde was centered around agriculture, with the cultivation of corn, beans, and squash playing a crucial role in sustaining the population. The Ancestral Puebloans developed sophisticated irrigation techniques, including the construction of reservoirs and check dams to manage water resources. They also practiced dry farming, taking advantage of the natural rainfall and the unique topography of the region. The ability to grow and store surplus food allowed the population to thrive and support a complex society.

In addition to agriculture, the Ancestral Puebloans of Mesa Verde engaged in a variety of other activities that supported their way of life. They were skilled artisans, creating pottery, textiles, and tools from local materials. Pottery from Mesa Verde is particularly notable for its intricate designs and high quality, reflecting a deep cultural and artistic tradition. The people also engaged in trade with neighboring regions, exchanging goods such as turquoise, shells, and feathers for items they could not produce locally.

The religious and ceremonial life of the Ancestral Puebloans was deeply intertwined with their daily activities. The kivas, which were central to their spiritual practices, served as places for rituals, meetings, and social gatherings. The construction of these kivas, often with elaborate masonry and symbolic features such as sipapus (small holes in the floor that represented the portal through which their ancestors emerged), reflects the importance of religion and community cohesion in their society. The great kiva, a larger and more elaborate version of the standard kiva, was used for significant communal events and religious ceremonies.

The abandonment of Mesa Verde in the late 13th century remains one of the great mysteries of North American archaeology. Several factors likely contributed to the decision to leave, including environmental changes, resource depletion, social upheaval, and external pressures from neighboring groups. A prolonged drought during this period would have made agriculture increasingly difficult, leading to food shortages and potentially exacerbating social tensions. Additionally, the depletion of local resources, such as timber and game, may have forced the inhabitants to seek more sustainable living conditions elsewhere.

Despite the abandonment of Mesa Verde, the descendants of the Ancestral Puebloans continued to thrive in other regions of the American Southwest. The Pueblo peoples of today, including the Hopi, Zuni, and other groups, maintain cultural and spiritual connections to Mesa Verde, viewing it as an ancestral homeland. These modern Pueblo communities continue to preserve and celebrate the traditions, languages, and practices passed down through generations, ensuring that the legacy of Mesa Verde remains alive.

The rediscovery of Mesa Verde in the late 19th century by European-American explorers and archaeologists brought the site to the attention of the wider world. In 1888, a pair of ranchers, Richard Wetherill and Charlie Mason, stumbled upon the cliff dwellings while searching for stray cattle. Their discovery sparked significant interest, leading to more systematic explorations and excavations. The work of early archaeologists, such as Gustaf Nordenskiöld, who conducted some of the first scientific excavations at Mesa Verde, helped to document and preserve the site for future study.

The establishment of Mesa Verde National Park in 1906 marked a significant milestone in the preservation and protection of the site. President Theodore Roosevelt signed the legislation creating the park, recognizing its historical and cultural significance. Since then, Mesa Verde has been managed by the National Park Service, which has undertaken extensive efforts to conserve and interpret the site for the public. These efforts include stabilizing the cliff dwellings, conducting ongoing archaeological research, and providing educational programs for visitors.

Today, Mesa Verde National Park attracts hundreds of thousands of visitors each year, offering a unique opportunity to explore the ancient cliff dwellings and learn about the Ancestral Puebloan culture. The park features a variety of trails, guided tours, and interpretive exhibits that provide insights into the history and significance of the site. Visitors can explore iconic locations such as Cliff Palace, Balcony House, and Long House, experiencing firsthand the ingenuity and resilience of the people who built and inhabited these remarkable structures.

Chapter 43: Ta Prohm

Ta Prohm, a stunning temple complex located in the Angkor region of Cambodia, is one of the most famous and iconic temples built during the Khmer Empire. Its enduring allure comes from the unique interplay between nature and architecture, where massive tree roots intertwine with ancient stone structures, creating a breathtaking and enigmatic landscape. Ta Prohm is part of the larger Angkor Archaeological Park, which includes numerous other significant temples such as Angkor Wat and Bayon, but it stands out due to its distinctive appearance and the deliberate decision to leave it in a relatively unrestored state, allowing visitors to experience it much as it was found by European explorers in the 19th century.

The temple of Ta Prohm was originally named Rajavihara, which means "Royal Monastery." It was commissioned by King Jayavarman VII in the late 12th century as a Mahayana Buddhist monastery and university. Jayavarman VII, one of the most powerful and prolific rulers of the Khmer Empire, was known for his extensive building projects, many of which were dedicated to the worship of Buddha and aimed at serving the spiritual and educational needs of his people. Ta Prohm was one of his most ambitious constructions, reflecting his devotion to Buddhism and his desire to create a monumental legacy.

Ta Prohm was designed to be a large monastic complex, comprising numerous enclosures, courtyards, and towers. At its peak, it housed thousands of monks, priests, and lay attendants, serving as a center for religious and scholarly activities. The temple's layout follows a traditional Khmer architectural plan, with a central sanctuary surrounded by concentric galleries and courtyards. The central sanctuary, which originally housed a statue of Prajnaparamita, the personification of wisdom, was the spiritual heart of the complex. This statue, believed to have been modeled after the king's mother, symbolized the king's devotion to his parents and his Buddhist faith.

The architecture of Ta Prohm is characterized by its intricate carvings and bas-reliefs, which depict various scenes from Buddhist mythology and the everyday life of the Khmer people. These carvings are a testament to the high level of artistic skill and craftsmanship achieved by the Khmer builders. They include depictions of apsaras (celestial dancers), devatas (deities), and scenes from the life of the Buddha. The walls and doorways are adorned with elaborate floral and geometric patterns, enhancing the temple's aesthetic appeal and spiritual ambiance.

One of the most remarkable features of Ta Prohm is its symbiotic relationship with the surrounding jungle. When the temple was rediscovered by French explorers in the 19th century, it had been largely reclaimed by nature. Towering trees, primarily the silk-cotton tree (Ceiba pentandra) and the strangler fig (Ficus gibbosa), had taken root in the structures, their massive roots spreading over the walls and through the galleries. This natural takeover has created a unique and hauntingly beautiful environment, where the ancient stonework and the encroaching vegetation seem to exist in a delicate balance. The trees, some of which rise over 30 meters, provide a canopy that casts dappled light over the ruins, adding to the mystical atmosphere of the site.

The decision to maintain Ta Prohm in a semi-ruined state was made by the École française d'Extrême-Orient (EFEO), the French institution responsible for the conservation of Angkor. Unlike other temples in the Angkor complex, which have undergone significant restoration, Ta Prohm was left largely as it was found, with minimal intervention to ensure structural stability and visitor safety. This approach allows visitors to experience the temple much as it appeared when it was first encountered by Western explorers, preserving the sense of wonder and discovery.

Conservation efforts at Ta Prohm have focused on stabilizing the ruins and preventing further damage from the encroaching vegetation.

While the roots of the trees are integral to the site's aesthetic and historical significance, they also pose a threat to the structural integrity of the temple. Conservationists have employed various techniques to manage this delicate balance, including reinforcing walls, installing unobtrusive support structures, and carefully trimming the roots to prevent excessive damage. These efforts aim to preserve the temple's unique character while ensuring its long-term survival.

Ta Prohm's appeal extends beyond its architectural and natural beauty; it also holds significant cultural and historical value. The temple serves as a testament to the grandeur and sophistication of the Khmer Empire, which, at its height, was one of the most advanced and powerful civilizations in Southeast Asia. The construction of Ta Prohm and other monumental projects during Jayavarman VII's reign highlights the empire's achievements in engineering, architecture, and art, as well as its deep spiritual and religious devotion.

In addition to its historical importance, Ta Prohm has captured the imagination of people worldwide, partly due to its appearance in popular media. It gained international fame as a filming location for the 2001 movie "Lara Croft: Tomb Raider," starring Angelina Jolie. The film showcased the temple's otherworldly beauty and introduced it to a global audience, further solidifying its status as an iconic and must-visit destination.

Visiting Ta Prohm offers a unique and immersive experience, allowing travelers to step back in time and explore the remnants of a once-thriving civilization. The site's evocative atmosphere, with its towering trees and moss-covered ruins, provides a stark contrast to the more restored and manicured temples in the Angkor complex. Walking through the narrow passageways and expansive courtyards, visitors can sense the passage of time and the relentless power of nature, which has both preserved and transformed this ancient monument.

The significance of Ta Prohm extends to the local communities and the broader Cambodian society. The temple is a source of national pride and cultural identity, representing the enduring legacy of the Khmer Empire and its contributions to the region's history and heritage. It also plays a vital role in the local economy, attracting tourists from around the world and providing employment and income for many Cambodians.

In recent years, there has been a growing recognition of the need to balance tourism with conservation. The influx of visitors to Ta Prohm and other sites in the Angkor complex has placed pressure on the fragile structures and the surrounding environment. To address these challenges, the Cambodian government and international organizations have implemented measures to manage visitor numbers, enhance infrastructure, and promote sustainable tourism practices. These efforts aim to protect the cultural and natural heritage of Ta Prohm while ensuring that future generations can continue to enjoy and appreciate its unique beauty.

Chapter 44: The Viking Ring Fortresses

The Viking Ring Fortresses, also known as Trelleborg fortresses, are a series of fortifications constructed during the late 10th century in Denmark and southern Sweden. These impressive structures, attributed to the reign of King Harald Bluetooth, are among the most fascinating and mysterious remnants of the Viking Age. Their precise geometric design, strategic locations, and the uniformity of construction across multiple sites indicate a high level of planning and organization, showcasing the Vikings not only as fierce warriors and seafarers but also as skilled engineers and administrators.

The most well-known of these fortresses is the Trelleborg near Slagelse on the island of Zealand in Denmark. Discovered in 1934, Trelleborg is a perfect circle, 137 meters in diameter, with a rampart constructed from earth and timber, surrounded by a ditch. The fortress is divided into four quadrants by two perpendicular streets, and each quadrant contains four large longhouses, believed to have been barracks for the garrison stationed there. The design is remarkably uniform, with precise angles and measurements, indicating that the builders employed advanced surveying techniques.

In addition to Trelleborg, several other ring fortresses have been discovered, including Aggersborg, Fyrkat, Nonnebakken, and Borrering in Denmark, and another Trelleborg near Trelleborg in southern Sweden. Each of these fortresses shares the same distinctive circular design and internal layout, suggesting that they were part of a coordinated construction project overseen by central authority. This uniformity also implies that the fortresses served a specific strategic purpose, likely related to military defense and control over the surrounding regions.

Aggersborg, located near the Limfjord in northern Jutland, is the largest of the ring fortresses, with a diameter of 240 meters. It contains the remains of 48 longhouses arranged in a similar grid pattern to those at Trelleborg. The size and location of Aggersborg suggest that it played a crucial role in controlling the northern trade routes and protecting the region from potential invaders. Fyrkat, near Hobro in northern Jutland, is another well-preserved fortress, with a diameter of 120 meters and containing 16 longhouses. Fyrkat's strategic position at the head of the Mariager Fjord indicates its importance in controlling access to the inland waterways.

The precise purpose of the Viking ring fortresses has been the subject of much scholarly debate. Some theories suggest that they were constructed as military strongholds to defend against external threats, such as the Germans to the south or rival Viking chieftains. The fortresses' strategic locations, often near important waterways or trade routes, support this theory. The presence of large numbers of weapons and other military artifacts at these sites further indicates their use as garrisons for trained warriors.

Another theory posits that the ring fortresses were administrative centers designed to exert royal control over the Danish kingdom. King Harald Bluetooth, who is credited with unifying Denmark and converting the Danes to Christianity, may have constructed these fortresses to consolidate his power and enforce his authority across the realm. The uniformity and precision of the fortresses suggest a centralized planning and construction process, indicative of a strong and organized government. The fortresses could have served as bases for royal officials, who administered justice, collected taxes, and maintained order in the surrounding areas.

In addition to their military and administrative functions, the ring fortresses likely played a role in facilitating trade and commerce. Their strategic locations near important trade routes would have allowed the control and protection of commercial activities, ensuring the safe passage of goods and merchants. The presence of large granaries and storage facilities within the fortresses suggests that they also functioned as centers for the collection and redistribution of agricultural produce and other resources.

The construction of the ring fortresses required a significant investment of resources and labor, indicating the presence of a well-organized society capable of mobilizing and directing large-scale building projects. The fortresses were constructed using a combination of timber, earth, and stone, with the ramparts typically built from layers of turf and clay, reinforced with wooden palisades. The ditches surrounding the ramparts were often filled with water, providing an additional layer of defense. The longhouses within the fortresses were constructed from timber, with thatched roofs and wattle-and-daub walls.

Archaeological excavations at the ring fortresses have provided valuable insights into the daily lives of the inhabitants. The remains of workshops, smithies, and other craft facilities indicate that the fortresses were centers of production and industry. Artifacts such as tools, weapons, pottery, and jewelry found at the sites suggest a high level of craftsmanship and a thriving material culture. The presence of imported goods, such as glass beads and ceramics from the Rhineland, indicates that the fortresses were connected to broader trade networks extending across Europe.

The discovery of burial sites at the ring fortresses provides further evidence of their significance. The graves often contain rich grave goods, including weapons, tools, and personal items, reflecting the high status of the individuals buried there. Some of the graves are of women, suggesting that the fortresses were not solely male military establishments but also included families and households. The presence of Christian symbols in some of the graves indicates the influence of Christianity during this period, reflecting the religious transformation initiated by King Harald Bluetooth.

The decline and abandonment of the ring fortresses towards the end of the 10th century remain somewhat mysterious. Several factors likely contributed to their decline, including changes in military strategy, shifts in trade routes, and political upheavals. The fortresses may have lost their strategic importance as the threats they were designed to counter diminished or as new political dynamics emerged. The construction of other fortifications and settlements in the region may have also played a role in their abandonment.

Despite their decline, the Viking ring fortresses left a lasting legacy in the history of Denmark and the Viking Age. They stand as a testament to the architectural and engineering prowess of the Vikings, as well as their ability to organize and mobilize resources on a large scale. The fortresses also provide valuable insights into the political, military, and economic structures of the Viking society, highlighting the complexity and sophistication of the early medieval Scandinavian world.

In recent years, the ring fortresses have become important archaeological and cultural heritage sites, attracting scholars, tourists, and history enthusiasts from around the world. Ongoing research and excavations continue to shed light on their construction, function, and significance, contributing to our understanding of the Viking Age. Efforts to preserve and interpret these sites have made them accessible to the public, allowing visitors to explore and appreciate the rich history and legacy of the Vikings.

The Viking ring fortresses represent a remarkable chapter in the history of Scandinavia, embodying the ingenuity, ambition, and complexity of the Viking Age. Their impressive construction, strategic significance, and enduring mystery make them a subject of fascination and study, offering a window into the world of the Vikings and their remarkable achievements. As we continue to uncover and explore these ancient fortresses, we gain a deeper appreciation for the legacy of the Vikings and their impact on the history of Europe.

Chapter 45: The Baths of Caracalla

The Baths of Caracalla, also known as Thermae Antoninianae, stand as one of the grandest and most impressive remnants of ancient Rome. Constructed under the reign of Emperor Caracalla, between 212 and 216 AD, these public baths were among the largest and most luxurious bathing complexes of the Roman Empire. Spanning an area of 25 hectares, they exemplify the Roman dedication to public leisure, architectural innovation, and urban planning. The Baths of Caracalla were not merely a place for bathing; they were a monumental public space that offered social, cultural, and recreational activities, reflecting the grandeur and sophistication of Roman society.

The construction of the Baths of Caracalla was a colossal undertaking, requiring vast resources and labor. The site chosen for the baths was located on the southeastern side of Rome, near the Via Appia. The complex was designed to accommodate thousands of visitors at a time, catering to the needs of the populous city. The baths were part of Caracalla's efforts to gain public favor and secure his legacy, following the assassination of his father, Emperor Septimius Severus, and his brother, Geta, whom he had killed in a bid to consolidate his power.

The architectural design of the Baths of Caracalla was both functional and aesthetically grand. The complex was arranged symmetrically, with a central bathing area flanked by various auxiliary facilities. The main bathing block was built on a massive platform and included a series of large halls and chambers, each serving different purposes. The primary rooms were the frigidarium (cold room), tepidarium (warm room), and caldarium (hot room), designed to offer a sequential bathing experience that began with a cold plunge, moved through warm, and culminated in the hot baths.

The frigidarium was a vast hall with a vaulted ceiling and large pools of cold water. It was often the starting point for bathers who sought to refresh themselves before moving on to the warmer rooms. The tepidarium, a transitional chamber, was heated to a moderate temperature and served as a preparation room for the caldarium. The caldarium was the most impressive of all, featuring a massive domed roof, large hot water pools, and underfloor heating systems known as hypocausts. The hypocaust system, a hallmark of Roman engineering, involved raising the floors on pillars to allow hot air from furnaces to circulate beneath, thereby heating the floors and walls.

In addition to the main bathing rooms, the Baths of Caracalla included numerous other facilities that contributed to the complex's multifunctional nature. There were gymnasiums for physical exercise, libraries for reading and study, and lecture halls for intellectual pursuits. The complex also housed shops, food stalls, and gardens, making it a vibrant social hub. The palaestra, or exercise courtyards, were open-air spaces where visitors could engage in sports and physical training, reflecting the Roman emphasis on physical fitness.

One of the most remarkable features of the Baths of Caracalla was its extensive and elaborate decoration. The interiors were adorned with opulent materials, including marble, mosaics, and frescoes. The floors were covered with intricate mosaic patterns depicting mythological scenes, geometric designs, and natural motifs. The walls were lined with marble panels and decorated with frescoes and stucco work. Sculptures and statues of gods, heroes, and emperors were strategically placed throughout the complex, adding to the grandeur and providing a visual feast for visitors.

The exterior of the Baths of Caracalla was equally impressive. The massive brick and concrete structure were covered with marble and stucco, giving it a majestic appearance. The complex was surrounded by porticoes and colonnades, which provided shaded walkways for visitors. The entrance was marked by a grand staircase and an imposing façade, creating a sense of awe and anticipation for those entering the baths. The extensive use of arches, vaults, and domes showcased the advanced engineering and architectural skills of the Roman builders.

The water supply for the Baths of Caracalla was another feat of Roman engineering. The baths were supplied with water from the Aqua Marcia, one of Rome's major aqueducts. A dedicated branch of the aqueduct, the Aqua Antoniniana, was constructed to bring a continuous and abundant flow of water to the complex. The water was stored in large cisterns and distributed through a network of pipes to the various pools and fountains within the baths. The efficient management of water supply and drainage was crucial for the operation of such a large facility, reflecting the sophistication of Roman urban infrastructure.

The Baths of Caracalla were more than just a place for bathing; they were a center of social and cultural life in Rome. The complex provided a space where people from all walks of life could come together, relax, and engage in various activities. It was a place for socializing, conducting business, and enjoying leisure time. The presence of libraries and lecture halls indicated that the baths also served as a venue for intellectual and cultural pursuits, making them an important part of the city's public life.

Despite their grandeur and significance, the Baths of Caracalla were in use for only about 300 years. The decline of the Roman Empire and the subsequent invasions by barbarian tribes led to the deterioration and eventual abandonment of the baths. In the 6th century, the Ostrogoths cut the water supply to Rome, rendering the baths unusable. Over the centuries, the complex fell into ruin, and its valuable materials were scavenged for other building projects. The marble and sculptures were particularly prized and were reused in various constructions throughout the medieval and Renaissance periods.

The rediscovery and excavation of the Baths of Caracalla in the 19th and 20th centuries brought renewed interest and appreciation for this magnificent ancient site. Archaeologists and historians have worked to uncover and preserve the remains of the baths, revealing the extent of their architectural and engineering prowess. Today, the ruins of the Baths of Caracalla stand as a testament to the grandeur of Roman civilization and its contributions to architecture, engineering, and urban planning.

The Baths of Caracalla continue to captivate visitors and scholars alike. The sheer scale and complexity of the site, along with its historical significance, make it a must-see destination for anyone interested in ancient Rome. The surviving mosaics, frescoes, and architectural elements provide a glimpse into the opulence and sophistication of Roman public baths. The site is also used for cultural events, such as concerts and performances, bringing new life to this ancient space and connecting the past with the present.

Chapter 46: The Palace of Knossos

The Palace of Knossos, situated on the island of Crete, is one of the most significant archaeological sites in the world, representing the zenith of the Minoan civilization, which flourished between approximately 2000 and 1400 BC. This grand palace complex, often associated with the legendary King Minos and the myth of the Minotaur, stands as a testament to the architectural and cultural achievements of the Minoans. The site, extensively excavated and partially reconstructed by British archaeologist Sir Arthur Evans in the early 20th century, offers a window into the sophistication, complexity, and artistry of an ancient civilization that greatly influenced the course of Mediterranean history.

The origins of the Palace of Knossos trace back to around 1900 BC, during the early Minoan period. The palace underwent multiple phases of construction and renovation, reflecting the changing needs and tastes of its inhabitants. The complex eventually covered approximately 20,000 square meters, making it the largest Bronze Age archaeological site on Crete. Its layout is characterized by a labyrinthine arrangement of rooms, corridors, and courtyards, which has led some to associate it with the mythological labyrinth of the Minotaur. Central to the palace's design was the Grand Courtyard, a large open space that served as the focal point for public ceremonies, gatherings, and possibly religious rituals.

Architecturally, the Palace of Knossos is remarkable for its advanced construction techniques and innovative features. The Minoans utilized ashlar masonry, employing large, carefully cut stones to create sturdy and aesthetically pleasing structures. The palace's multi-story buildings were supported by a system of wooden columns and beams, which provided both strength and flexibility in the event of an earthquake. The columns, a distinctive feature of Minoan architecture, were tapered downwards and painted in vibrant colors, adding to the visual appeal of the palace.

The complex was designed with a sophisticated drainage and water management system, one of the most advanced of its time. This included indoor plumbing with flush toilets, elaborate drainage systems to handle rainwater, and aqueducts to supply fresh water from nearby springs. The existence of such amenities underscores the Minoans' engineering prowess and their concern for hygiene and comfort.

One of the most striking aspects of the Palace of Knossos is its vibrant and elaborate frescoes. These wall paintings, which adorned many of the palace's rooms and corridors, depict a wide range of scenes, from religious and ceremonial activities to depictions of nature and everyday life. The frescoes are notable for their dynamic compositions, vivid colors, and attention to detail, showcasing the Minoans' artistic skills and their appreciation for natural beauty. Notable examples include the "Bull-Leaping Fresco," which illustrates a ceremonial activity involving athletes vaulting over bulls, and the "Prince of the Lilies," a depiction of a young man adorned with flowers.

The Palace of Knossos also served as a major religious center, reflecting the importance of religion in Minoan society. Numerous shrines and sacred spaces have been identified within the complex, indicating that the palace was not only a political and administrative hub but also a spiritual center. The Minoans worshipped a pantheon of deities, often represented by symbols such as the double axe (labrys) and the horns of consecration, both of which have been found in abundance at Knossos. The central courtyard may have been used for religious ceremonies and processions, emphasizing the close integration of religious practice with daily life.

Economically, the Palace of Knossos functioned as a central hub for the surrounding region. It contained extensive storage facilities, including large pithoi (storage jars), used for storing agricultural produce such as grain, olive oil, and wine. This indicates that the palace played a crucial role in the collection, storage, and redistribution of goods, supporting a complex economy based on agriculture, trade, and craft production. Artifacts such as pottery, tools, and luxury items found at the site provide evidence of both local production and long-distance trade, connecting the Minoans with other contemporary civilizations across the Mediterranean.

The administrative functions of the palace are evidenced by the discovery of numerous Linear A tablets, inscribed with the still-undeciphered script used by the Minoans. These tablets likely recorded economic transactions, inventories, and other bureaucratic matters, highlighting the advanced administrative capabilities of Minoan society. The presence of elaborate workshops within the palace complex suggests that it was also a center for various crafts, including pottery, metalworking, and textile production.

The social and political structure of Minoan society, as reflected in the Palace of Knossos, remains a subject of scholarly debate. The layout of the palace, with its numerous rooms, courtyards, and specialized areas, suggests a highly organized and hierarchical society. The central position of the throne room, with its elaborate decorations and the presence of a ceremonial throne, indicates the existence of a ruling elite. This elite likely included a king or queen, religious leaders, and high-ranking officials, who oversaw the administration of the palace and the surrounding region.

Despite its grandeur, the Palace of Knossos faced numerous challenges over its long history. The site was affected by several natural disasters, including earthquakes and fires, which led to multiple phases of destruction and rebuilding. Around 1450 BC, the palace suffered a catastrophic event, possibly related to the volcanic eruption on the nearby island of Thera (Santorini), which led to significant destruction. Although the palace was partially rebuilt and continued to be used, its influence waned, and it was eventually abandoned around 1300 BC.

The rediscovery of the Palace of Knossos in the early 20th century by Sir Arthur Evans marked a turning point in the study of Minoan civilization. Evans' extensive excavations revealed the complexity and sophistication of the site, bringing to light the achievements of a civilization that had been largely forgotten. However, his reconstruction efforts, which involved the liberal use of reinforced concrete to rebuild and restore parts of the palace, have been the subject of controversy. While these reconstructions have made the site more accessible and visually striking, they have also raised questions about the accuracy and authenticity of the restored structures.

Today, the Palace of Knossos remains one of the most important and visited archaeological sites in Greece. It continues to captivate scholars, tourists, and history enthusiasts with its rich history and the mysteries it still holds. The site provides invaluable insights into the Minoan civilization, shedding light on their architectural, artistic, and cultural achievements. Ongoing archaeological research and conservation efforts aim to preserve this remarkable site for future generations, ensuring that the legacy of the Minoans endures.

Chapter 47: Temple of the Sun

The Temple of the Sun, also known as the Sun Temple, is a renowned archaeological site that serves as a testament to the architectural and astronomical prowess of ancient civilizations. One of the most famous Sun Temples is located in Konark, Odisha, India. This temple, often referred to as the Konark Sun Temple, was constructed in the 13th century by King Narasimhadeva I of the Eastern Ganga Dynasty. Designed in the shape of a colossal chariot, the temple is dedicated to the Hindu Sun God, Surya. It is an exceptional example of the Kalinga architectural style and is recognized for its intricate carvings and detailed sculptures.

The temple's architecture is symbolic and represents a colossal chariot with twelve pairs of wheels, pulled by seven horses. These wheels are intricately carved and are not merely decorative; they also function as sundials. The precision with which these sundials were created demonstrates the advanced understanding of time and astronomy by the ancient builders. The temple is aligned along the east-west axis, allowing the first rays of the sunrise to strike the principal entrance, a feature that underscores the significance of the Sun God in this sacred space.

The Konark Sun Temple is renowned for its exquisite stone carvings, which adorn every surface of the structure. These carvings include depictions of various deities, celestial beings, animals, and scenes from everyday life. One of the most remarkable aspects of these carvings is the depiction of various human and divine figures in dynamic poses, showcasing a high level of artistry and craftsmanship. The sculptures also reflect the social, cultural, and religious practices of the time, offering valuable insights into the life and beliefs of the people who built the temple.

Another notable Sun Temple is located in the ancient city of Machu Picchu, Peru. This temple, also known as the Intihuatana or

"Hitching Post of the Sun," was a significant ceremonial center for the Inca civilization. The temple is situated on a hilltop, and its strategic location allowed the Incas to observe celestial events and perform important religious rituals. The Intihuatana stone, a carved rock pillar within the temple, was used as an astronomical clock or calendar. During the solstices, the shadow of the pillar would align perfectly with certain points, helping the Incas to mark the changing seasons and plan agricultural activities accordingly.

The Sun Temple at Abu Simbel in Egypt is another iconic example of ancient sun-worship architecture. Built by Pharaoh Ramses II in the 13th century BCE, this temple complex was designed to align with the sun in such a way that twice a year, the sun's rays would penetrate the sanctuary and illuminate the statues of the gods seated at the back wall. This precise alignment was an incredible engineering feat, considering the limited technological resources available at the time. The temple's facade is adorned with colossal statues of Ramses II, and its interior walls are covered with elaborate carvings depicting the pharaoh's military victories and religious ceremonies.

In Mesoamerica, the ancient city of Teotihuacan in present-day Mexico is home to the Pyramid of the Sun, one of the largest structures of its kind in the Western Hemisphere. This pyramid, built around 200 CE, was part of a vast complex that included residential, ceremonial, and administrative buildings. The Pyramid of the Sun was aligned with the setting sun on the day of its construction, demonstrating the importance of solar worship in Teotihuacan culture. The pyramid's massive size and the precise alignment of its corners with the cardinal points indicate a sophisticated understanding of astronomy and engineering among the builders.

The Great Zimbabwe in southern Africa is another site where the Sun Temple plays a crucial role. The Great Enclosure, the largest stone structure at the site, is believed to have served as a religious and ceremonial center. Within the Great Enclosure, there is a conical tower that is thought to have been a symbol of the sun and fertility. The alignment of the tower with the rising and setting sun during certain times of the year suggests that the people of Great Zimbabwe had a deep connection to solar cycles and used the sun as a guide for their agricultural and ritualistic practices.

In Cambodia, the ancient temple complex of Angkor Wat is renowned for its architectural grandeur and astronomical significance. Originally dedicated to the Hindu god Vishnu, Angkor Wat was later transformed into a Buddhist temple. The temple's layout is based on a mandala, representing the cosmic order, and its central tower symbolizes Mount Meru, the mythical home of the gods. The alignment of Angkor Wat with the equinoxes and solstices indicates that the Khmer builders had a profound understanding of celestial movements. During the spring equinox, the sun rises directly over the central tower, creating a spectacular visual effect that reinforces the temple's sacred significance.

The Sun Temple of the ancient city of Palenque in Mexico is another remarkable example of sun-worship architecture. Known as the Temple of the Sun, this structure is part of the larger Palenque complex, which was an important center of the Maya civilization. The temple's design includes a series of hieroglyphic inscriptions and intricate carvings that depict scenes from Maya mythology and history. The alignment of the temple with the solar cycles played a crucial role in the Maya calendar and religious ceremonies, highlighting the importance of the sun in their culture.

The Sun Temple of Heliopolis in ancient Egypt, also known as the Great Temple of Ra, was one of the most significant religious sites in the ancient world. Located in the city of Heliopolis, which was a major center for the worship of the sun god Ra, the temple complex included a massive obelisk and numerous other structures dedicated to various deities. The obelisk, which stood as a symbol of the sun's rays, was aligned with the solstices and served as a focal point for religious rituals and ceremonies. The temple's design and alignment demonstrate the central role of solar worship in ancient Egyptian religion and culture.

The Sun Temple of Qorikancha in Cusco, Peru, was the most important temple in the Inca Empire. Dedicated to Inti, the Inca sun god, Qorikancha was a stunning example of Inca architecture and engineering. The temple's walls were covered in sheets of gold, which reflected the sun's rays and symbolized the divine connection between the emperor and the sun god. The precise alignment of Qorikancha with the solstices and other celestial events allowed the Incas to use the temple as an astronomical observatory, helping them to develop an accurate calendar and plan agricultural activities.

The Sun Temple of Arkaim, located in the southern Ural region of Russia, is a lesser-known but fascinating example of ancient sun-worship architecture. Arkaim was a Bronze Age settlement and archaeological site that included a circular fortification and a central temple complex. The alignment of the temple with the cardinal points and the solstices suggests that the inhabitants of Arkaim had a sophisticated understanding of astronomy. The temple's design, with its circular layout and concentric rings, reflects the importance of the sun and celestial cycles in the spiritual and daily life of the ancient people of Arkaim.

The Sun Temple of Stonehenge in England is one of the most iconic prehistoric monuments in the world. This ancient stone circle, believed to have been constructed around 3000 BCE, has long been associated with sun worship and astronomical observation. The alignment of Stonehenge with the solstices, particularly the summer solstice when the sun rises directly over the Heel Stone, indicates that the monument was used to mark important solar events. The precise positioning of the stones and the complexity of the construction suggest that the builders of Stonehenge had a deep knowledge of astronomy and engineering.

The Sun Temple of Mesa Verde in Colorado, USA, is an example of a sun-worship site built by the Ancestral Puebloans. The Mesa Verde cliff dwellings, which date back to the 12th century, include a number of ceremonial structures known as kivas. These kivas, particularly the Sun Temple, were used for religious rituals and community gatherings. The alignment of the Sun Temple with the solstices and other celestial events demonstrates the importance of the sun in Ancestral Puebloan culture and their advanced understanding of astronomy.

The Sun Temple of Chichen Itza in Mexico is another remarkable example of Mesoamerican sun-worship architecture. The Temple of Kukulkan, also known as El Castillo, is a step pyramid that was used for both religious and astronomical purposes. The pyramid's design includes a series of terraces and staircases that create a shadow effect during the equinoxes, resembling a serpent slithering down the steps. This alignment with the solar cycles highlights the significance of the sun in Maya cosmology and the advanced astronomical knowledge of the builders.

The Sun Temple of Tikal in Guatemala is one of the largest and most important ceremonial structures of the ancient Maya civilization. The temple, also known as Temple IV, stands as a testament to the architectural and astronomical achievements of the Maya. The alignment of Temple IV with the solstices and equinoxes allowed the Maya to use the temple as an observatory, helping them to develop an accurate calendar and conduct religious ceremonies. The intricate carvings and hieroglyphic inscriptions on the temple's walls provide valuable insights into Maya mythology and history.

The Sun Temple of Abu Ghurab in Egypt is another significant site dedicated to the worship of the sun god Ra. This temple, located near the pyramids of Giza, was built during the 5th Dynasty of the Old Kingdom. The temple complex included a large obelisk and an altar where rituals and offerings were made to the sun god. The alignment of the temple with the solar cycles underscores the central role of sun worship in ancient Egyptian religion and the advanced understanding of astronomy among the builders.

The Sun Temple of Uaxactun in Guatemala is a notable example of ancient Maya sun-worship architecture. The site includes a series of temples and observatories that were used for religious ceremonies and astronomical observations. The alignment of the temples with the solstices and other celestial events highlights the importance of the sun in Maya culture and the sophisticated astronomical knowledge of the builders. The hieroglyphic inscriptions and carvings at Uaxactun provide valuable information about Maya mythology, history, and religious practices.

The Sun Temple of Pachacamac in Peru was a major religious center for the pre-Inca and Inca civilizations. Located near Lima, the temple complex included a series of structures dedicated to the worship of the sun god Inti. The alignment of the temple with the solstices and other celestial events allowed the inhabitants to use the site for astronomical observations and religious ceremonies. The intricate carvings and architectural features of the Sun Temple at Pachacamac reflect the advanced engineering skills and spiritual beliefs of the ancient people of the region.

These Sun Temples, scattered across different continents and cultures, reflect a universal reverence for the sun and its significance in the daily and spiritual lives of ancient civilizations. Each temple, with its unique architectural features and astronomical alignments, offers valuable insights into the advanced knowledge and religious practices of the people who built them. The enduring legacy of these temples continues to inspire and intrigue historians, archaeologists, and visitors from around the world.

Chapter 48: Temple of Hera

The Temple of Hera, also known as Heraion, is one of the most significant sanctuaries dedicated to the goddess Hera in ancient Greek religion. There are several prominent temples dedicated to Hera, but among the most famous are the Temple of Hera at Olympia and the Temple of Hera at Samos. These temples stand as testaments to the architectural ingenuity and religious devotion of the ancient Greeks.

The Temple of Hera at Olympia, known as the Heraion of Olympia, is one of the oldest and most significant temples in Greece. Constructed around 600 BCE, this temple is a prime example of early Doric architecture. Originally, the temple was a wooden structure that was later rebuilt in stone. The Heraion was part of the sanctuary of Olympia, which also housed the famous Temple of Zeus and the ancient Olympic Games. The temple's layout is a peripteral design, featuring a rectangular floor plan surrounded by a single row of columns, with six columns on the short sides and sixteen on the long sides.

The temple's interior was divided into three sections: the pronaos (front porch), the cella (main chamber), and the opisthodomos (rear porch). The cella housed the cult statues of Hera and Zeus, although Hera's statue was the primary focus. The statue of Hera was a seated figure made of wood, while the statue of Zeus, which was later added, was made of gold and ivory. The temple's altars, where rituals and sacrifices were conducted, were located outside the main structure, in line with typical Greek religious practices.

One of the unique features of the Heraion at Olympia is its blend of architectural styles, reflecting the transition from wooden to stone construction. The columns, for instance, exhibit variations in style and proportion, indicating that they were replaced or modified over time. This blending of styles provides valuable insights into the evolution of Greek temple architecture. The temple also featured a rich array of decorative elements, including terracotta roof tiles and ornate acroteria (decorative roof ornaments). These embellishments not only enhanced the temple's aesthetic appeal but also demonstrated the artistic skills and creativity of the ancient builders.

The Temple of Hera at Samos, also known as the Heraion of Samos, is another significant sanctuary dedicated to the goddess. The Heraion of Samos is located on the island of Samos, near the ancient city of Pythagoreion. This temple was one of the largest and most impressive structures of its time. The sanctuary was originally established in the 8th century BCE, but the most prominent phase of construction took place in the 6th century BCE, under the rule of the tyrant Polycrates. The temple at Samos was designed by the renowned architect Rhoikos, and it featured an innovative dipteral layout, with a double row of columns surrounding the cella. This design created a grand and imposing structure that reflected the importance of the goddess Hera in the local religious practices.

The Heraion of Samos was distinguished by its monumental scale and elaborate decoration. The temple measured approximately 55 meters in length and 25 meters in width, with 24 columns on the long sides and 8 columns on the short sides. The columns were characterized by their slender proportions and elegant capitals, which were adorned with intricate floral and geometric motifs. The cella housed a colossal cult statue of Hera, made of wood and adorned with gold and ivory. The statue was positioned on a high pedestal, emphasizing the goddess's divine status and making it visible to worshippers from a distance.

The temple complex at Samos also included a large altar, where rituals and sacrifices were performed. The altar was a focal point of the sanctuary, and it was often decorated with offerings and votive objects. These offerings included a wide range of items, such as pottery, jewelry, and figurines, which were dedicated to Hera by her worshippers. The sanctuary also featured a sacred way, a processional route that led from the city of Pythagoreion to the temple. This route was lined with statues and other monuments, creating a grand approach to the temple and enhancing its sacred atmosphere.

The Heraion of Samos was not only a religious center but also a hub of cultural and political activity. The sanctuary hosted a variety of festivals and events, including athletic competitions, musical performances, and theatrical productions. These events attracted visitors from across the Greek world, fostering a sense of community and shared cultural identity. The sanctuary also served as a venue for diplomatic gatherings and negotiations, reflecting its importance as a center of political power and influence.

In addition to these two prominent temples, Hera was worshipped in numerous other sanctuaries throughout the Greek world. One notable example is the Temple of Hera at Paestum, located in southern Italy. Paestum, originally known as Poseidonia, was a Greek colony founded in the 7th century BCE. The Temple of Hera at Paestum, built around 550 BCE, is one of the best-preserved examples of Doric architecture. The temple features a peripteral design, with nine columns on the short sides and eighteen columns on the long sides. The columns are characterized by their sturdy proportions and simple, fluted shafts. The temple's cella housed a cult statue of Hera, and the exterior was adorned with metopes and triglyphs depicting mythological scenes.

The Temple of Hera at Paestum also includes a number of unique architectural features, such as a double row of columns in the pronaos and a separate adyton (inner sanctum) at the rear of the cella. These features reflect the temple's dual function as both a place of worship and a storage facility for valuable offerings and votive objects. The temple's construction and decoration demonstrate the wealth and cultural sophistication of the Greek colonists who settled in southern Italy.

The worship of Hera extended beyond mainland Greece and the Greek colonies, influencing various aspects of Mediterranean culture. Hera was revered as a powerful and protective deity, associated with marriage, childbirth, and the family. Her sanctuaries often served as centers of social and communal life, where individuals and families sought her blessings and protection. The rituals and ceremonies dedicated to Hera were diverse and varied, ranging from simple offerings and prayers to elaborate processions and festivals. These practices underscored the importance of Hera in the daily lives of the ancient Greeks and their deep reverence for the goddess.

The temples dedicated to Hera were not only religious centers but also architectural masterpieces that showcased the ingenuity and creativity of ancient Greek builders. The use of stone, the development of the Doric and Ionic orders, and the incorporation of intricate decorative elements all contributed to the grandeur and beauty of these structures. The temples' alignment with natural features and celestial events also reflected the Greeks' deep connection to the natural world and their belief in the divine order.

Archaeological excavations at the sites of these temples have provided valuable insights into the construction techniques, artistic traditions, and religious practices of the ancient Greeks. The remains of the temples, along with the artifacts and votive offerings discovered at the sites, have helped scholars reconstruct the history and significance of these sacred spaces. The study of these temples continues to shed light on the complex and multifaceted nature of ancient Greek religion and culture.

The legacy of the Temple of Hera and other ancient sanctuaries dedicated to the goddess continues to inspire and captivate modern audiences. These structures stand as enduring symbols of the ancient Greeks' devotion to their gods and their extraordinary achievements in art, architecture, and engineering. The temples dedicated to Hera, with their monumental scale, intricate decoration, and profound religious significance, remain among the most important and impressive monuments of the ancient world.

Chapter 49: The Temple of Solomon

The Temple of Solomon, also known as the First Temple, is a central and highly significant structure in Jewish history and tradition. It was constructed in ancient Jerusalem and served as the primary place of worship for the Israelites and the dwelling place of the Ark of the Covenant. The temple's construction is attributed to King Solomon, the son of King David, during the 10th century BCE, and it stood as a symbol of Israelite religion, culture, and national identity.

The origins of the Temple of Solomon can be traced back to King David, who initially conceived the idea of building a permanent dwelling for the Ark of the Covenant. According to biblical accounts, David amassed materials for the temple's construction but was not permitted by God to build it himself due to his history of warfare and bloodshed. Instead, the task was entrusted to his son Solomon, who ascended the throne of Israel around 970 BCE. Solomon's reign was marked by peace and prosperity, providing the ideal conditions for undertaking such an ambitious project.

The construction of the Temple of Solomon began around the fourth year of Solomon's reign, approximately 966 BCE. The site chosen for the temple was Mount Moriah, a location of great religious significance in Jerusalem. This site was traditionally believed to be the place where Abraham had prepared to sacrifice his son Isaac in obedience to God's command. The selection of this site underscored the temple's deep connection to the patriarchal heritage and the covenant between God and the Israelites.

The building process was a monumental task that required vast resources and labor. According to the Bible, King Solomon enlisted the help of Hiram, the king of Tyre, to supply materials and skilled craftsmen. Hiram provided cedar and cypress timber from the forests of Lebanon, as well as skilled laborers such as stonecutters, carpenters, and metalworkers. The workforce included tens of thousands of

Israelites and foreign laborers who toiled for seven years to complete the temple. The materials used in the construction were of the highest quality, including gold, silver, bronze, and precious stones, which adorned various parts of the temple, enhancing its splendor and majesty.

The design and layout of the Temple of Solomon were highly elaborate and meticulously planned. The temple was constructed according to divine instructions given to Solomon, with dimensions and specifications that held symbolic significance. The structure was divided into three main sections: the Porch (Ulam), the Holy Place (Hekhal), and the Holy of Holies (Debir). The Porch served as the entrance to the temple and was adorned with two massive bronze pillars named Jachin and Boaz, each standing about 27 feet tall. These pillars were intricately decorated with capitals, chains, and pomegranates, symbolizing strength and stability.

The Holy Place, the main hall of the temple, was a rectangular chamber measuring approximately 60 feet long, 30 feet wide, and 45 feet high. This area was the primary space for daily worship and religious rituals. It housed several sacred objects, including the Altar of Incense, the Table of Showbread, and the Golden Lampstand (Menorah). The walls of the Holy Place were lined with cedar panels, carved with figures of cherubim, palm trees, and open flowers, and overlaid with gold, creating a dazzling interior that reflected the glory and majesty of God.

The innermost sanctum of the temple, the Holy of Holies, was a square chamber measuring about 30 feet on each side. This sacred space was separated from the Holy Place by a thick curtain or veil, known as the Parochet. The Holy of Holies was the most revered and restricted area of the temple, accessible only to the High Priest and only once a year on Yom Kippur, the Day of Atonement. The primary purpose of this chamber was to house the Ark of the Covenant, the most sacred artifact of the Israelites. The Ark, a wooden chest overlaid with gold, contained the stone tablets of the Ten Commandments, a pot of manna, and Aaron's rod that had budded. The lid of the Ark, known as the Mercy Seat, was flanked by two golden cherubim with outstretched wings, symbolizing God's divine presence.

The temple's exterior was equally magnificent, featuring a series of courtyards, gates, and ancillary structures. The outer court, known as the Court of the Gentiles, was open to all visitors, including non-Israelites. This area provided space for gatherings, teaching, and commerce. The inner court, reserved for Israelites, included the Court of the Women, the Court of Israel, and the Court of the Priests. The Court of the Priests contained the Altar of Burnt Offerings, a large bronze altar used for animal sacrifices, and the Bronze Sea, a massive basin for ritual purification. Surrounding the temple were various chambers and storerooms used for storing offerings, sacred utensils, and the priestly garments.

The dedication of the Temple of Solomon was a momentous event, marked by elaborate ceremonies and festivities. According to the biblical account, Solomon invited all the leaders and elders of Israel to Jerusalem for the dedication. The Ark of the Covenant was brought into the temple with great reverence and placed in the Holy of Holies. As the Ark was installed, the temple was filled with a cloud symbolizing the divine presence, and Solomon offered a lengthy prayer of dedication, invoking God's blessing upon the temple and the people of Israel. The dedication ceremonies included numerous sacrifices, feasting, and celebrations that lasted for several days.

The Temple of Solomon served as the religious, cultural, and political center of Israelite life for nearly four centuries. It was the focal point of worship and pilgrimage, where Israelites from all over the kingdom would come to offer sacrifices, seek atonement, and celebrate religious festivals such as Passover, Shavuot, and Sukkot. The temple also played a crucial role in the administration of justice and governance, as the king and the priesthood were closely linked to its functioning.

Despite its grandeur and significance, the Temple of Solomon faced several challenges and periods of decline. The kingdom of Israel experienced political instability, invasions, and internal strife, which impacted the temple's upkeep and religious practices. One of the most significant threats came from the Babylonian Empire, which emerged as a dominant power in the Near East. In 586 BCE, under the leadership of King Nebuchadnezzar II, the Babylonians besieged Jerusalem, breached its walls, and destroyed the city. The Temple of Solomon was looted, set on fire, and razed to the ground, marking the end of the First Temple period. The destruction of the temple and the subsequent exile of the Jewish people to Babylon were catastrophic events that deeply affected the Israelite community and their religious identity.

The memory of the Temple of Solomon continued to hold immense significance for the Jewish people during their exile and after their return to Jerusalem. The hope and aspiration to rebuild the temple became a central theme in Jewish prayers, prophecies, and religious texts. This aspiration was eventually realized with the construction of the Second Temple, initiated by the Persian king Cyrus the Great and completed under the leadership of Zerubbabel, a descendant of David, and the high priest Joshua. The Second Temple, although less grand than Solomon's Temple, became the new center of Jewish worship and played a crucial role in the religious and cultural life of the Jewish people until its destruction by the Romans in 70 CE.

The legacy of the Temple of Solomon extends beyond its historical and religious significance. It has been a source of inspiration for various religious traditions, including Judaism, Christianity, and Islam. In Judaism, the temple represents the ultimate place of divine presence and worship, and the hope for its restoration remains a core element of Jewish eschatology. In Christianity, the temple is seen as a precursor to the concept of Jesus as the ultimate high priest and the embodiment of God's presence. In Islam, the site of the temple, known as the Haram al-Sharif or the Noble Sanctuary, is revered as a holy place, housing the Al-Aqsa Mosque and the Dome of the Rock.

The Temple of Solomon has also influenced art, architecture, and literature throughout history. Its descriptions in biblical texts have inspired countless artistic depictions, from medieval manuscripts and Renaissance paintings to modern-day illustrations and films. The architectural elements and symbolism of the temple have been studied and incorporated into various religious and cultural structures around the world.

In addition to its religious and cultural impact, the Temple of Solomon continues to be a subject of archaeological and historical interest. Excavations and research in Jerusalem and its surroundings have provided valuable insights into the ancient city's layout, construction techniques, and daily life during the First Temple period. These findings have enriched our understanding of the historical context and significance of the temple and its role in the broader history of the ancient Near East.

The Temple of Solomon stands as a monumental symbol of ancient Israelite religion, culture, and identity. Its construction, destruction, and enduring legacy reflect the profound spiritual and historical significance it holds for the Jewish people and the broader religious and cultural heritage of humanity. The temple's story is a testament to the enduring power of faith, the resilience of a people, and the timeless quest for a connection with the divine.

Chapter 50: The Lighthouse of Alexandria

The Lighthouse of Alexandria, also known as the Pharos of Alexandria, was one of the Seven Wonders of the Ancient World and an extraordinary feat of engineering and architecture. Located on the small island of Pharos in the harbor of Alexandria, Egypt, it was constructed during the reign of Ptolemy II Philadelphus (283–246 BCE). The lighthouse was designed to guide sailors safely into the busy harbor of Alexandria, which was a crucial center of trade and culture in the ancient Mediterranean world. Standing at an estimated height of around 100 to 130 meters (330 to 430 feet), the Lighthouse of Alexandria was one of the tallest man-made structures in the world for many centuries.

The idea of building a lighthouse at Alexandria is traditionally attributed to Ptolemy I Soter, the founder of the Ptolemaic Kingdom in Egypt, although the actual construction was carried out under his son, Ptolemy II Philadelphus. The city of Alexandria, founded by Alexander the Great in 331 BCE, quickly grew into a major hub of commerce, scholarship, and culture. Its strategic location on the Mediterranean coast made it a vital link between Egypt and the rest of the Hellenistic world. The bustling port of Alexandria required a beacon to help navigate ships safely through the perilous waters and into the harbor, especially at night and during adverse weather conditions.

The architect Sostratus of Cnidus is often credited with the design and construction of the lighthouse, although there is some debate among historians about his precise role. According to legend, Sostratus inscribed his name on the lighthouse, hidden beneath a dedication to Ptolemy, to ensure his legacy would be remembered. The construction of the lighthouse was a massive undertaking that required significant resources, skilled labor, and advanced engineering techniques.

The Lighthouse of Alexandria was built using large blocks of light-colored stone, primarily limestone and granite, which were quarried locally and transported to Pharos Island. The structure consisted of three main tiers: a square base, a cylindrical middle section, and a smaller circular tower at the top. The design was both functional and aesthetically pleasing, with each tier serving a specific purpose. The square base, measuring approximately 30 meters (98 feet) on each side, provided a stable foundation for the towering structure and housed various rooms, including storage areas and living quarters for the lighthouse keepers.

The cylindrical middle section, which rose above the base, was the most prominent part of the lighthouse. This section featured a spiral ramp or staircase that allowed access to the upper levels. The walls of the middle section were adorned with decorative elements, such as columns and statues, showcasing the artistic and architectural sophistication of the Hellenistic period. The cylindrical design helped to reduce wind resistance and provided structural stability, allowing the lighthouse to withstand the harsh maritime environment.

At the top of the cylindrical section was the smaller circular tower, which housed the lighthouse's beacon. The beacon consisted of a large open flame, typically fueled by wood or oil, which was visible from a great distance. To enhance the visibility of the light, the flame was reflected and magnified using polished bronze mirrors or metal plates. These mirrors concentrated the light into a focused beam, which could be seen by ships approaching Alexandria from far out at sea. The circular tower also featured a colonnade with an observation platform, providing a panoramic view of the surrounding area.

The entire structure was capped with a statue, often identified as a representation of Zeus or Poseidon, the Greek god of the sea. This statue added to the grandeur and symbolic significance of the lighthouse, emphasizing its role as a guardian of sailors and a symbol of the city's maritime prowess. The lighthouse's beacon was crucial for navigation, especially during the night and in foggy or stormy conditions. Mariners relied on the light to avoid the dangerous reefs and shoals near the coast and to find their way safely into the harbor. The lighthouse not only served a practical function but also stood as a monumental symbol of Alexandria's wealth, power, and cultural achievements.

The Lighthouse of Alexandria quickly became renowned throughout the ancient world for its impressive height, innovative design, and vital role in maritime navigation. It was a source of pride for the people of Alexandria and a marvel for visitors and traders from distant lands. The lighthouse's fame and significance were such that the term "pharos" became synonymous with lighthouses in many languages, reflecting its iconic status.

The lighthouse's enduring legacy is also reflected in various historical texts and accounts from ancient writers and travelers. The geographer Strabo, who visited Alexandria in the late 1st century BCE, provided one of the earliest descriptions of the lighthouse, noting its towering presence and the brilliance of its beacon. The Roman author Pliny the Elder, writing in the 1st century CE, also mentioned the lighthouse in his "Natural History," praising its grandeur and the skill of its builders. These accounts, along with other historical records, have helped to preserve the memory of the Lighthouse of Alexandria and its significance in the ancient world.

Despite its remarkable construction and enduring legacy, the Lighthouse of Alexandria faced numerous challenges over the centuries. The structure was subjected to natural wear and tear, as well as the destructive forces of earthquakes. Alexandria is located in a seismically active region, and several significant earthquakes struck the area during the lighthouse's existence. Historical records indicate that major earthquakes in the 10th and 14th centuries caused severe damage to the lighthouse, ultimately leading to its collapse. By the late 14th century, the lighthouse was no longer standing, and its ruins were gradually submerged beneath the waters of Alexandria's harbor.

In the centuries following its collapse, the remains of the Lighthouse of Alexandria were repurposed for other construction projects. Some of the stones from the lighthouse were used to build the Citadel of Qaitbay, a defensive fortress constructed in the 15th century on the site of the former lighthouse. The citadel, which still stands today, serves as a historical reminder of the lighthouse's presence and significance.

Modern archaeological efforts have sought to uncover the remains of the Lighthouse of Alexandria and gain a better understanding of its construction and impact. Underwater excavations in the waters around Pharos Island have revealed numerous artifacts and architectural fragments that are believed to be remnants of the lighthouse. These discoveries have provided valuable insights into the lighthouse's design, materials, and the advanced engineering techniques used by its builders.

The Lighthouse of Alexandria remains an enduring symbol of human ingenuity, architectural achievement, and the importance of maritime navigation. Its towering presence and brilliant beacon guided countless sailors to safety and facilitated the flow of trade and culture throughout the ancient Mediterranean world. The lighthouse's legacy continues to inspire and captivate people around the world, serving as a testament to the remarkable accomplishments of ancient civilizations and their enduring impact on history.

Epilogue

As we conclude our journey through the ancient world, we find ourselves standing at the intersection of past and present, reflecting on the incredible legacies left behind by our ancestors. The structures we have explored in "World's Oldest Structures: Famous Landmarks of the Ancient Times" are not merely relics of a bygone era; they are enduring symbols of human ingenuity, resilience, and aspiration.

These ancient landmarks, whether carved from stone, molded from mud bricks, or constructed from timber, tell us stories of diverse cultures and peoples who, despite the vast distances and epochs separating them, shared a common drive to leave a mark on the world. They built for the gods, for their rulers, for their communities, and for future generations, creating monuments that have withstood the test of time.

In our modern age, where technology evolves at a breathtaking pace and the digital realm often overshadows the physical, these ancient structures remind us of the power of human hands and minds. They urge us to look beyond our screens and rediscover the tangible, the enduring, and the magnificent achievements of those who came before us.

Each stone, column, and archway speak of a time when the world was both vast and mysterious, when knowledge was shared through oral traditions and inscribed in symbols. The ruins and remains we have studied serve as bridges to those distant times, connecting us to the artisans, laborers, priests, and rulers who once walked the earth.

As we walk away from this exploration, we carry with us not just the knowledge of these incredible structures, but also a deeper appreciation for the heritage they represent. We are reminded that history is not just a series of dates and events but a tapestry woven from countless lives, dreams, and accomplishments. It is a testament to what humanity can achieve through creativity, cooperation, and sheer determination.

Our journey through the world's oldest structures may have come to an end, but the stories they hold continue to live on. They inspire us to preserve our heritage, to honor the past, and to strive for a future where our own creations might one day stand as testaments to our time.

As you close this book, may you carry with you a sense of wonder and curiosity, a desire to explore further, and a deep respect for the incredible feats of ancient engineering and artistry. The world is filled with treasures waiting to be discovered, and the echoes of history are all around us, inviting us to listen, learn, and marvel.

Thank you for joining us on this remarkable journey through the annals of ancient times. May the stories of these famous landmarks inspire you to seek out the wonders of the world, both old and new, and to appreciate the timeless human spirit that binds us all.

The End.